RARE BREED

The Entrepreneur, An American Culture

RARE BREED

The Entrepreneur,
An American Culture

William MacPhee

Probus Publishing Company
Chicago, Illinois

This publication is designed to provide accurate and authoritative
information in regard to the subject matter covered. It is sold with the
understanding that the publisher is not engaged in rendering legal,
accounting or other professional service. If legal advice or other expert
assistance is required, the services of a competent professional person
should be sought.

ISBN 0-917253-75-2

Printed in the United States of America

1 2 3 4 5 6 7 8 9 0

Acknowledgements

*T*he title, *Rare Breed,* is dedicated to Edward Marshall Boehm (1913-1969) in recognition of his accomplishments and contributions in the field of fine porcelain. He was a man of quality and integrity— in life and art. His porcelain creations are everlasting reminders of the "quest for the best" that *is* the American Spirit.

To you, Mr. Boehm, we dedicate this work, and we thank you. You truly personified the Rare Breed, America's great natural resource.

We are grateful to Helen Boehm, wife of the late artist, for her contribution to this book.

This work is the combined effort of thirteen entrepreneurs who have dedicated their lives to perpetuating their species. By sharing their stories, often emotionally, they have contributed significantly to the rejuvenation of the entrepreneurial spirit, the driving force behind America's success and continued vitality.

I thank you Mary K. Short and the Short/Wiley family for your friendship, tenacity, love, encouragement, and devotion, which were *vitally* needed for me to accomplish this book particularly in the face of significant obstacles.

One thanks one's parents with achievements inspired by their input and direction, and by sustaining their example, in one's endeavors.

Acknowledgements

On January 24, 1987, the entrepreneurs interviewed in this book and 200 of their invited guests convened in Phoenix, Arizona for "An Evening With the Rare Breed." Each entrepreneur was presented with a leather bound, gold leaf copy of *Rare Breed* which was numbered and signed by all thirteen entrepreneurs. Also, nine copies of the special edition were auctioned and $21,000 was raised for various charities. The success of this event was due in large part to Mr. Eugene Rondeau and Ms. Nancy Casper of American Airlines, who coordinated the transportation, and to the staff at Pointe Tapatio Cliffs Resort.

Special appreciation goes to Al and Susan Attee, whose efforts made the unveiling of *Rare Breed* a total success.

This effort faced numerous obstacles and at times I wondered if it would be completed. Its completion was due, in large part, to the professionalism, conviction, and support of Phil Kaplan, my attorney; Brent Leslie, my CPA with Arthur Young; and some very special people: David Hayes, Mark and Laura Yarbrough, Allen and Susan Attee, and Jim and Linda Short. These people certainly are Rare Breeds.

Table of Contents

Chapter 1

The Rare Breed

The Rare Breed

*T*he twentieth century, and particularly the part of the century in which we live, is decidedly anti-heroic. In a world dulled by mediocrity and the constant intrusion of mass media, we have come to regard heroism with skepticism, accepting it only as parody and the stuff of fiction. Yet, ironically, the need for real flesh-and-blood heroes has not diminished in our culture, and this is no less true for our business culture. The hero is an important rallying point and role model, a tangible example to others that feats of incredible difficulty can be accomplished, that seemingly insurmountable obstacles can be overcome, and that strongly held beliefs and traditional values are far worthier human characteristics than cynicism and the self-absorbed obsessions of the "me-generation".

The Rare Breed is about true American heroes of the business world. They are, each and every one of them, entrepreneurs *par exellence* whose individual business accomplishments are unique and nothing short of remarkable and whose positive influence reaches well beyond their particular enterprises and personal successes.

The Rare Breed is also about rediscovering and rejuvenating the American entrepreneurial spirit, which had lain dormant in this country for so many years, in the face of stiff foreign

3

competition, inflexible numbers-oriented management styles and laxness in product and service quality.

When we first undertook to write this book, our intention was to explore the specific characteristics that led to the considerable successes of some of this country's most remarkable entrepreneurs. To this end, we specifically selected thirteen entrepreneurs in twelve distinct industries to reveal the special qualities they possess that enabled them to achieve as they have. We found that although they are truly distinct personalities they nonetheless share many common characteristics and many of the same values and attitudes about business and life in general.

Rare Breed is a biographical exploration of the human side of enterprise, with all its personal joys of success and travails of failure, to which we now turn.

Our Rare Breed Entrepreneurs

Mary Kay Ash—Founder and Chairwoman of Mary Kay Cosmetics. In addition to producing an excellent cosmetics line, Mary Kay is highly regarded for the humanistic work environment she has established at her company, which encourages God, family, and Mary Kay Cosmetics, in that order. Her people skills, which are set forth in her book, *On People Management* (Warner Books, 1984) are held in high esteem internationally. Mary Kay also is respected for her optimistic and motivating leadership style, which, as you will read in our interview with her, she developed while overcoming incredible personal hardships over the course of her life.

Melvyn Bell—Founder, Chairman, and CEO of Environmental Systems Company (ENSCO), which is considered the largest, the most safety conscious, and the most efficient incinerator waste treatment company in America. Bell is highly respected for his tenacity in purchasing financially weak companies and successfully turning them around. He is reknowned for his ability to identify and attract brilliant people to his team and to motivate them and direct their collective energies to the successful achievement of mutual goals.

Helen Boehm—Co-founder and Chairwoman of the Edward Marshall Boehm Company, the producer of the world's finest hard-paste porcelain figurines. She is respected for her exceptional promotional abilities which have enabled her, within the period of a decade, to launch her late husband's porcelain work into the international art arena, a task that normally would be expected to take several decades. Every U.S. President since Eisenhower has given Boehm porcelain as gifts of State.

J.B. Hunt—Founder and Chairman of J.B. Hunt Transport, one of the youngest and most profitable major commercial trucking companies in America. Hunt is known for his excellent business timing, often courageously taking positions contrary to popular trends. He also has applied his highly successful management style and business acumen to industries other than trucking, including banking.

Paul Klipsch—Founder and Chairman of Klipsch and Associates, a company with the reputation for building the finest stereo speakers in the world. Although Japan dominates the electronics industry worldwide, Klipsch is able to export 30 percent of its production, with much of it going to Japan. Japanese electronic manufacturers, in fact, are known to use Klipsch speakers to test their own products. "Your stereo system is only as good as your speakers!"

Robert Mondavi—Founder and President of Robert Mondavi Winery, producer of some of the world's finest wines. He is highly regarded for the technological advances he has applied to winemaking and for his innovative and participative management style, which relies on full contributions from all his people. He sees this as a key to the success and credibility of Mondavi wines around the world.

John L. Morris—Founder and President of Bass Pro Shops, the world's largest retail sports outlet and one of Missouri's most popular tourist attractions. Bass Pro is known for the excellent full-color fishing catalogue it issues, considered by many professional sports fisherman to be the "industry bible." Morris is also respected for his ability to successfully manage three quite different types of businesses; retail outlets, catalogue sales, and boat manufacturing.

J.R. (Jack) Simplot—Founder and Chairman of the J.R. Simplot Company, which is the largest U.S. potato processor, the third largest U.S. cattle operation, the largest U.S. phosphate fertilizer producer, and a recent entry into the highly competitive electronic microchip industry. Simplot is highly regarded for his ability to manage waste efficiently and develop creative and profitable commercial applications for its re-use.

Gerald Smith—Co-founder of Allied Bankshares, one of the nation's most profitable commercial banks. Smith is respected for his ability to attract and motivate people and for his acute marketing savvy, through which he was able to focus the bank's efforts on a select and profitable banking market niche. He is known for his eagerness and ability to instill the entrepreneurial spirit in his employees, most of whom are stockholders in the bank.

Donald Tyson—Chairman of Tyson Foods Inc., the world's largest poultry processor. Tyson is respected for leading his company through the most protracted industry downturn ever, and having it emerge as the world's leading poultry processor. Tyson Foods was ranked first among Fortune 500 companies for return on equity in 1985 and was eighth over a ten-year period.

Roy Weatherby—Founder and Chairman of Weatherby, Inc., makers of the highest quality, safest, and most elegant sports firearms, which are often given as gifts of State by the U.S. government. Weatherby is credited with introducing the most innovations to sports firearms in the past 100 years.

Forrest and Nina Wood—Founders of Wood Manufacturing, the producers of Ranger boats, which are considered the world's leading sports fishing boats. Ranger boats are highly regarded for their safety, durability, effectiveness, and styling. The Woods are credited with numerable contributions to the multi-billion-dollar sports fishing industry.

Twelve Key Entrepreneurial Characteristics

In preparing to write *The Rare Breed,* we commissioned students at Stanford, Harvard and Vanderbilt Universities to conduct research on the characteristics that are important to entrepreneurial success. We also surveyed 1,500 entrepreneurs by mail, soliciting their assessments of the traits they felt primarily shaped their business careers and lives.

Our reasons for conducting the research and survey were two-fold. First, we wanted to see what differences there were, if any, between the theoretical, conventionally held perceptions of the traits that lead to entrepreneurial success and those of real-world entrepreneurs. And, secondly, we wanted to use the results of the studies to establish a framework for our interviews with the thirteen entrepreneurs interviewed for the book.

One interesting thing we discovered in our research was that many of the entrepreneurial characteristics uncovered in the student research — including such traits as "decisive" and "well organized" — were not considered vital by the practicing entrepreneurs in our survey. We further confirmed these differences in the interviews with our 13 Rare Breed entrepreneurs, one of whom indicated that most of the traits identified by the student research were more appropriate for a book entitled "Effective Management" than in one about entrepreneurship. Thus the 12 traits that we decided on, which are listed below, were derived primarily from our survey of entrepreneurs and further confirmed by our interviews with the 13 entrepreneurs we introduced earlier in the chapter.

As you review the 12 traits, please keep in mind that the list is not meant to be all encompassing, nor do all the traits apply to all entrepreneurs to the same degree. The list merely reflects the traits that our sample of entrepreneurs felt were the most important in shaping their business successes.

The 12 characteristics are:

1. Vision	7. Independence
2. Desire to Achieve	8. Competitiveness
3. Self-Confidence	9. Possessiveness
4. Desire for Recognition	10. High Energy and Drive
5. Opportunistic	11. Promotional Orientation
6. Ability to Make Sacrifices	12. Resourcefulness

Below is a brief explanation of each characteristic as it relates to the interviews in the chapters that follow:

Vision

This trait was ranked the most important by our entrepreneur survey respondents and was discussed most frequently by our 13 Rare Breed interviewees.

Entrepreneurs have always been thought of as having that rare talent of being able to "see" things in their environment — unexploited market opportunities, unmet consumer needs, new products, and so forth — that others cannot.

Entrepreneurs have described to us their ability to see in their mind's eye the end result of what they want to achieve. If it is a new product they plan to develop, for instance, they actually can envision the physical characteristics of the product and can see customers buying the product and using it. Even before starting their companies, they are able to picture what their company will be and can see themselves managing employees and running operations that exist only in their imaginations.

This trait has been compared to daydreaming with a purpose and is not unlike the visualization or simulation techniques regularly used by successful performers and athletes. Many pro golfers, for example, will visualize a golf shot before actually hitting the ball. They will picture themselves making a perfect swing, seeing the club head strike the ball and watching the ball in flight landing on the green and rolling to a spot next to the hole. This mental simulation helps them program their minds and bodies to accomplish the task at hand, according to Dr. Dennis Waitley, who has conducted extensive research on the subject for his work *The Psychology of Winning*.

Being able to visualize the successful result of their efforts helps entrepreneurs to overcome the assorted obstacles they may encounter along the way. It gives them the confidence and provides them with the energy and driving force to work their way through seemingly insurmountable problems and to buck discouraging trends and contrary thinking to reach their visualized goals.

Desire to Achieve

Most successful entrepreneurs are goal oriented and have a strong desire to achieve the demanding objectives they establish for themselves.

Although all the entrepreneur survey respondents and Rare Breed interviewees agreed that money or wealth is a source of motivation, most contend that it was not their primary motivation. In most cases the accumulation of money is most valued for its ability to provide the entrepreneur with the independence to pursue his or her other goals. According to Nina and Forrest Wood, "Money is how you keep score, but once a minimal level was achieved for our independence to pursue our boat ideas, it was no longer an issue. The issue became accomplishment and watching our people at Ranger grow individually and collectively."

Some entrepreneurs talked about their desire to achieve simply for its own sake — J. R. Simplot, for instance, spoke of the appeal to him of "the hunt and the chase" — but others had more definite goals in mind, such as making the best product, providing the best service, being the most innovative, or developing the best people.

Self-Confidence

The very act of undertaking an entrepreneurial venture requires an incredible amount of optimism and confidence in one's abilities to survive and thrive in the world of business. It is this characteristic, coupled with their vision of the end results, that enables entrepreneurs to achieve their goals in the face of opposition. Entrepreneurs often can be quite alone in their business pursuits. They often choose to disregard "conventional wisdom" in achieving their goals, and thereby, often are questioned and even ridiculed by others. It is confidence in one's self and in one's goals and an optimistic attitude that help them endure. According to J. R. Simplot "nothing will ever be attempted if all possible objections must first be overcome."

Desire for Recognition

This is the entrepreneur's primary reward for his or her efforts, risks and sacrifices. As we touched on earlier in the discussion of achievement, money is not the principal motivator of entrepreneurs. They want to be recognized as doing the undoable, as providing the best products and service, employing the best people, and so forth.

According to Helen Boehm, "When President Eisenhower commissioned Boehm to create the porcelain 'Polo Player' as a gift of State for Queen Elizabeth and Prince Phillip, we finally gained the international recognition we worked for and deserved." This theme runs throughout our interviews: To build the best and to be number one. As Roy Weatherby said, "Ego and recognition for achievement are powerful driving forces. Everybody appreciates being recognized, but the entrepreneur thrives on it."

Opportunistic as to Luck and Timing

As Gary Player, the professional golfer, is quoted as saying, "Sure, luck is important, but the more I practice, the luckier I get." Most of the entrepreneurs we talked to readily admit the role that chance and timing played in their successes, but they also were quick to point out that they felt it was their ability to identify and act on a fortuitous event or circumstance that made the difference. According to Mary Kay Ash, "Luck and timing play a vital role in success, but equally important is the ability to capitalize on it." Helen Boehm adds "Luck and timing are one of God's great mysteries, but you must have the ability to seize the moment and then ride that horse through to the finish line." And, as J. R. Simplot puts it, "There are two kinds of people in this world, those that simply think about it and those that act. I act!"

Ability to Make Scarifices

All of our interviewees have had to make personal sacrifices to achieve their entrepreneurial goals. They all have exhibited an incredible capacity to overcome obstacles and endure personal hardships in order to reach their goals in business and life.

The life of Mary Kay Ash, for instance, illustrates her amazing ability to overcome difficult personal circumstances, particulary in her youth when she had to care for her dying father while her mother worked 16-hour days, seven days a week to provide food and shelter for the family. Helen Boehm came from a strong, large, Italian Catholic family, but sacrificed starting a family of her own, opting instead to focus all her energies on her vision for Boehm porcelains.

All our Rare Breed entrepreneurs sacrificed personal pleasures and private time, devoting large parts of their lives to developing their products and companies.

Forrest Wood, for one, told us how he sacrificed countless nights of sleep to deliver Ranger boats to customers. Often, after driving all night, he would shower immediately upon getting home and take his daughters to rodeos, where they actively competed. Roy Weatherby, who spent many 18- to 24-hour days developing and promoting his premier rifles, said, "I guess one of the greatest tragedies of my efforts was my sacrifice of

11

my family." Melvyn Bell of Environmental Systems Company adds, "I always thought everyone worked 80-hour weeks."

Independence

Entrepreneurs, by nature, are an independent lot. The world the entrepreneur tries to create for his or her enterprise is one that is free of restraint, interference, conventional wisdom, and, most of all, bureaucracy, all of which are considered to be stifling and counter productive forces to the entrepreneur. These people spend a good part of their lives in a battle for independence, attempting to gain and maintain as much control as possible over their destinies and those of their businesses.

Two areas that are particularly troublesome to the entrepreneurs we interviewed in terms of maintaining independence are government interference and the stock market.

A leading management consulting firm surveyed 2,000 corporate executives in 1985 and found that the majority of their time was spent dealing with government bureaucracy and regulation, all totally non-productive functions. We found that all of our 13 Rare Breed entrepreneurs do not rely on or want government regulation, subsidies or import quotas, not even when they might support or protect their businesses from competition. On the contrary, these individuals take pride in competing against and beating larger and more established domestic and foreign competitors.

Similarly, in the widely held public corporation, senior management's future is largely predicated on quarterly earnings reports, the assessments and recommendations of stock analysts, and the short-term, return-on-investment mentality of the stock market. Most entrepreneurs do not perform well when confronted with the restraints imposed upon them by the stock market. This is not to say that entrepreneurs do not take their companies public, many do. But it creates an environment that is counter to their nature. When asked if the publicly held nature of his company curtailed his actions, Melvyn Bell of ENSCO responded, "The public nature of our company has a direct and not always good impact on our efforts." Don Tyson on the other hand responded, "Hell no, I control over 50 percent of the stock!"

Competitiveness

Entrepreneurs have a strong innate desire to win. We touched on this briefly when discussing their desire to achieve. It is this trait that brings out their survival instincts. As Jack Simplot states, "Nobody, but nobody will undercut my price for phosphate and if the Japanese want to play hardball by discounting microchips, we will beat them and make money doing it." Don Tyson asks "Can you imagine suiting up for a football game with no opponent?" And he adds "When it comes to competition in the poultry industry, I am the most formidable son-of-a gun in the game!"

As you will read in the interviews that follow, our Rare Breed entrepreneurs thrive on competition and do not like to lose.

Possessiveness

The emergence of this trait in our interviews surprised us, since, before now, we had not heard it mentioned as a characteristic for entrepreneurial success.

All our Rare Breed entrepreneurs are very possessive about and protective of the things they feel are theirs, including their companies, the products or services their companies produce, and their employees. Entrepreneurs do not easily draw distinctions between themselves and their companies, which they tend to treat as extensions of themselves.

Possessiveness is a formidable trait; just how formidable it can be is in evidence in our interview with Jack Simplot. When fifty Maine potato brokers tried to corner the potato futures market, Simplot got tough. Likewise, when Lane Pocessing reneged on its offer to sell its poultry operation to Tyson Foods, Don Tyson responded by relentlessly pursuing them despite several legal maneuvers on Lane's part to avoid Tyson. Tyson's eventual acquisition of Lane made Tyson the largest poultry processor in the world.

Another aspect of this trait is the entrepreneur's paternalistic regard for his or her employees. All of our Rare Breed entrepreneurs expressed genuine feeling and caring for "our people," in many cases referring to them as family. This also is exhibited in the way these entrepreneurs encourage their employees to develop and the genuine delight they take seeing their people achieve their personal and professional goals. Below are some quotes from our interviews that reflect these sentiments:

"The most important thing is properly managing yourself so you can properly manage your people."

Mary Kay Ash
Mary Kay Cosmetics

"The greatest joy and the greatest heartbreak are people issues."

John Morris
Bass Pro Shops

"Businesses are an extension of the human expression."

Helen Boehm
Edward Marshall Boehm

"You must keep your organization young in spirit and my job is to keep the experience rich and rewarding."

J. B. Hunt
J. B. Hunt Transport

High Energy and Drive

The Rare Breed entrepreneur has enormous energy and endurance. Even after regularly working 18-hour days he or she still seems to have energy left over for other personal, civic, charitable and/or avocational pursuits.

In the beginning, of course, all energy is directed toward the survival of his or her company, with the entrepreneur performing all of the business' primary functions — sales, production, administration, etc. At some point, however, as the company matures and succeeds, the entrepreneur must cut back and redirect his or her energies. This is a difficult step for many entrepreneurs to take, but those that ignore and resist this evolution risk limiting their firms' potential to the level of their own capabilities. As Jack Simplot says "Transition is a difficult, and in some ways, never-ending process, but you have to let go and give free-reign; you simply can't do it all yourself."

Below are some quotes from our interviews, that illustrate how the roles of our Rare Breed entrepreneurs have evolved in their companies and how they have learned to share their responsibilities:

"My primary job is to create an environment where the entrepreneur will flourish."

> J. R. Simplot
> *J. R. Simplot Company*

"I let my people skin the cat their way."

> Don Tyson
> *Don Tyson Inc.*

"My job is to allocate the entrepreneurial spirit."

> **Gerald Smith**
> *Allied Bankshares*

"If central decision making worked we could run dictatorships. It doesn't work and we are collective in our decisions at Ranger Boats."

> **Forrest and Nina Wood**
> *Wood Manufacturing*

"Collective decision making solicits commitment, accomplishment, and provides my people with a feeling of ownership."

> **Robert Mondavi**
> *Robert Mondavi Winery*

"My primary job is to attract, rally, motivate, and reward the top people in the industry."

> **Melvyn Bell**
> *ENSCO*

Promotional Orientation

All of our Rare Breed entrepreneurs exhibited a unique instinct for promotion. They are constantly "on," promoting their companies or their products through themselves, or vice versa, every chance they can.

Mary Kay Ash, of course, is one obvious example, but as you read the interviews you will see others, including Helen Boehm's promotional strategy to associate her porcelain with royalty and the Wood's (Ranger Boats) and Morris' (Bass Pro Shops) strategy of associating themselves and their products with world class sports fishermen.

Resourcefulness

Entrepreneurs are extremely resourceful. They have had to be to survive and succeed. For most of them, especially in the beginning of their entrepreneurial careers, they had very few resources available in their businesses than did their larger and more established competitors. As a result they had to learn how to get more out of what they had — whether it be capital, land or labor. (Note: It was interesting and reassuring for us to see, by the way, that the business resource that our thirteen entrepreneurs assign the highest value to and spend the most time attending to is their people.)

On a more personal level, entrepreneurs also seem to be able to reach deeper into themselves than most and use every personal asset or resource they can muster to its fullest to overcome an obstacle and/or achieve a goal. In the interviews that follow, you will see excellent examples of just how resourceful our Rare Breed entrepreneurs have been in creating and building their enterprises.

Although we are well aware that overuse can very often drain the power of an otherwise useful metaphor, throughout our interviews we nonetheless frequently felt compelled to compare our Rare Breed entrepreneurs to the American eagle— the comparison was irresistable. The eagle's legendary power of sight, his independence, solitude and single minded pursuit of prey, his vigilance, his national symbolic value, even his scarcity call up images that are reminescent of the entrepreneur. We believe these same images will often come to mind as you read the pages that follow.

Chapter 2

Mary Kay Ash
of Mary Kay
Cosmetics

Mary Kay Ash of Mary Kay Cosmetics

"You Can Do It With People and Pride"

Mary Kay Ash is the Founder and Chairwoman of Mary Kay Cosmetics, a leading cosmetics manufacturer. The company, with over $300 million in revenues, sells to over 180,000 beauty consultants who work as independent contractors. The products are packaged as a facial care system and sold through in-home consulting sessions with no more than six invitees to encourage personalized consultation and prompt follow-up. According to Mary Kay, "We literally sell cosmetics, but we provide women with self-images so they feel better about themselves. That's our contribution to the world."

Ability to Overcome Obstacles

"Character is one of the most valuable human qualities and it is achieved by overcoming obstacles; we fall forward to success." That quote from the Mary Kay interview summarizes her life and her spirit. Mary Kay Cosmetics, Inc. was founded September 13, 1963, after Mary Kay had already retired from a successful sales career: this highly successful company was born from this remarkable woman's experience and an enduring dream. The dream was ambitious yet direct and clearly articulated:

"To begin a company that would give women the opportunity to do anything in the world if they had the desire and were smart enough to do it." But, the experiences that circumscribed and lead up to this dream were complex and arduous, as Mary Kay states, "I'll compare knees with anyone because I know what it's like to fall, crawl, and rebound."

The Mary Kay story clearly reveals that many of the entrepreneurial traits we identified in Chapter 1 are developed during childhood, often as coping mechanisms. As the individual matures and the survival traits are no longer needed, the tools developed are applied to his or her entrepreneurial endeavors. In Mary Kay's case, her self-confidence and character, built from overcoming numerous obstacles in childhood, imbued her with a "you can do it" conviction, which has enabled her to build one of the most successful cosmetic houses in the world.

Born in Hot Wells, Texas, sometime before 1930, (the exact date is known only to Mary Kay, and this writer's mother taught him better than to ask), Mary Kay's early years were spent nursing her father, who had tuberculosis. Her days were spent cleaning the house, cooking, helping her ailing father, and attending school while her mother managed a restaurant sixteen hours a day. From the beginning, her life was difficult, as she recalls, "When I was growing up, we had very little and I had to work hard. That experience made me want to excel and achieve. We had plenty of love and my mother always encouraged me by saying, 'You can do it, Mary Kay!' " "You can do it"—is the driving force behind Mary Kay Cosmetics, Inc.

The personal sacrifice and hardships she had to contend with and overcome, by her own assessment, forced Mary Kay into adulthood at the tender age of sixteen. In school, she achieved excellent grades, but as she recounts, "I was ready for college, but in those days there were no scholarships and we didn't have any money, so I couldn't go to school. So I did the next best thing, I got married. At seventeen, I married the Elvis Presley of Houston radio, who bowled me over." The marriage was to end in divorce and nearly shatter Mary Kay.

She recalls, "He was more concerned about his guitar and tuxedos than he was about me and the children, so I pursued a career in direct sales giving home demonstrations for Stanley Home Products, which also gave me family time." Within a year, Mary Kay, was recognized by Stanley as a top performer.

When her husband returned home after the war, he was greeted by Mary Kay's joy at having saved enough money for a down payment on a house. Her enthusiasm abruptly vanished, however, when he informed her that, while in the service, he had been living with another woman, who was now seven months pregnant, and he wanted a divorce. "That wrecked my life emotionally and resulted in what was diagnosed as rheumatoid arthritis. Actually, the symptoms were physical manifestations of my emotional breakdown." This eventually resulted in hospitalization and deep depression. After numerous examinations for the "arthritis," a doctor informed her that he felt the real problem was psychosomatic and recommended a balanced diet, rest, and, most important, he said, "You must face this trauma and *you can do it*." With these words, heard so many times before, and with her strong feeling of responsibility for her family, the arthritic symptoms disappeared after a year.

Some years later, Mary Kay left Stanley Home Products to join World Gift, which had a similar in-home sales approach. During this time, she began suffering from facial paralysis, which caused severe muscle spasms on the left side of her face. Initially, this too was diagnosed as psychosomatic. However, a series of tests revealed that she had a rare disease known as hemifacial spasms caused by a blood vessel wrapping around a cranial nerve. At that time, Dr. Gardner of the Cleveland Clinic was performing a high risk, exhausting surgery for the disease. He had performed eighteen such surgeries, lasting eight to twelve hours each, and nine had failed. After hours of tests, Dr. Gardner asked Mary Kay if she wanted the surgery. Her immediate reaction was, "Yes!" "The disease was emotionally debilitating and destroyed my self-confidence." Although the surgery was finally successful it nearly ended her life. Mary Kay awoke five days after the surgery in intensive care and remained hospitalized for two months.

These examples are testimony to Mary Kay's tenacity and ability to reach deep inside to overcome major obstacles and move forward. This trait—the character and stamina needed to pursue and achieve, to take risks, and to rebound—is very important to the entrepreneur and is what enables him or her to turn what would be failure for most into a learning/ winning experience. As Mary Kay says, "We fall forward to success by examining and learning from the bumps."

Competitiveness

While taking care of her ill father, Mary Kay often made personal sacrifices. On many occasions, she would clean and prepare the house for her father, missing her own breakfast so she could get to school on time. She would often stop by her friend Dorothy's house *en route* to school. Dorothy was quite pampered and had finicky breakfast habits, often turning her nose up at her "lavish meal," which Mary Kay often ended up eating. Mary Kay enjoyed Dorothy and her family and was often included in their family activities, such as vacations, which Mary Kay's family couldn't afford. Her relationship with Dorothy's family exposed her to the "good life," further wetting her appetite to achieve.

Mary Kay was routinely used as a role model for Dorothy by her parents, which in turn led to healthy competition between the two girls. Also, Mary Kay believed that her role model relationship to Dorothy was the key to being included in the family's activities. "Therefore, when Dorothy got A's, I had to get an A-plus, and when Dorothy sold nine May Fete tickets, I had to sell ten tickets. Whatever she did, I had to do more."

Another local family, knowing of her family situation, also took Mary Kay under their wing. Their daughter, Tillie was eight years older than Mary Kay. Mary Kay's competitiveness again made her strive to surpass the older girl's achievements in order to secure her relationship with the family.

In Dr. Dennis Waitley's work *The Psychology of Winning,* he emphasizes the importance of self-competition to avoid establishing standards representative of the non-winners who comprise about 90% of the population. Mary Kay is clearly among the 10%.

Occasionally, Mary Kay's competitiveness created problems. When Mary Kay and Dorothy graduated from high school, Dorothy entered Rice Institute. Mary Kay's family could not afford to send her to school and scholarships were nonexistent at the time. As she states in her autobiography, *Mary Kay,* "I did what I thought was the next best thing, I got married, to compete with Dorothy." This marriage, as we mentioned earlier, led to disaster for her leading her to declare, "I am convinced that competition is most productive when you are competing against yourself" (*Mary Kay,* page 17 — subsequent references to this source are abbreviated *M.K.*).

When Mary Kay joined Stanley Home Products, the company had a recruiting contest. "The one recruiting the most new sales people would be crowned 'Miss Dallas' and I was determined to win" (page 15, *M.K.*). At the time, she was holding three in-home sales presentations a day and she desperately needed the money that resulted from these presentations for her family. However, she sacrificed the sales, allowing other Stanley representatives to host the sales parties, so she could devote all her energies to winning the "Miss Dallas" title. Her sales dropped, because of her recruiting efforts, but in the long run, this short-term financial sacrifice was recouped several times over by her share of the commissions that were later earned by the new recruits she hired.

When the contest was over, Mary Kay won the "Miss Dallas" title and she states, "I was perfectly willing to give up my income for a week in order to earn the ribbon proclaiming me 'Miss Dallas'." These two traits of hers—self-competitiveness and the desire for recognition—that were born during her childhood were carried forward to her company. When she was first establishing her Mary Kay Cosmetics, she was careful to incorporate contests that encouraged self-competition and self-pacing and that resulted in a number of winners. "At Mary Kay, we never had a contest in which there was a first, second, and third prize and everyone else lost. I'd been through too many of those in my days with other direct sales organizations and I'd seen people step on each other to win a contest. This kind of competitiveness is so destructive to morale within an organization and we carefully avoid it altogether" (page 19, *M.K.*).

At Mary Kay Cosmetics, beauty consultants are encouraged to achieve through self-competition and their efforts are rewarded by commissions, awards, and other forms of recognition. The pinnacle of the year is Seminar, a three-day extravaganza in Dallas where workshops are held for the beauty consultants and their husbands. Here peer recognition overflows and achievement awards, such as diamonds, minks, and the "Mary Kay Pink" Cadillacs, are presented.

The diamond bumblebee award is presented to the leaders of various categories who are crowned "Queen." Mary Kay believes that the bumblebee is a symbol of self-competition and achievement because it can fly despite the well established fact that its ability to fly defies everything we know about aerodynamics. Fortunately for the bumblebee, it doesn't know that, and it goes right on flying. "We achieve by looking beyond perceived constraints and compete with ourselves," notes Mary Kay.

Vision, Optimism Resourcefulness

Vision and resourcefulness are powerful traits for entrepreneurs. These traits enable them to look beyond constraints and obstacles and to manage situations so that the odds are balanced in their favor. Entrepreneurs don't let things happen and then merely respond. They make things happen! They are risk takers in the sense that they know they won't achieve 100 percent of their goals, but they also know that their resourcefulness, vision, and self-confidence will result in more wins than losses.

Mary Kay took plenty of lumps, but she and her entrepreneurial peers have the ability to rebound from disappointment. Mary Kay is quick to deride such words as "maybe", "possibly," "someday," etc., that inhibit success. She believes firmly, as does Waitley, that pessimism and its manifestations, are self-imposed.

Mary Kay's resourcefulness is also demonstrated by her discipline in self-planning, goal setting, and putting her life and priorities in perspective. "By putting God first, family second, and career third, everything seems to work out" (page 56, *M.K.*). "I don't know exactly how it works, but God provides for the career."

In her autobiography, Mary Kay emphasizes time, discipline, and goal setting in the chapter titled "Plan Your Life Like Your Vacation." For Mary Kay, this process began in her youth when her time was limited, given her nursing duties, house chores, and school. The constant demands on her time continued through her marriage, and to cope, she began making a daily "do list." She writes her goals on paper, leaving copies in conspicuous places, such as her car and refrigerator. She also writes this list on her bathroom mirror. She lists her agenda for the next day and determines which items may be performed by others, delegates these, and puts the balance of the list into order of importance. She obviously believes in stretching her capabilities, but she is also a realist and her list usually consists of just six priority items. In her agenda, she puts the least interesting or hardest goal first in order to give it renewed attention and prevent it from influencing the rest of the day. By accomplishing the least desirous goal first, her day is left clean, without a cloud to blur her vision and divert her from her other goals.

She breaks her goals up into manageable segments in order to deal more effectively with the problems at hand. This approach is stressed in her company's corporate culture of planning, achievement, and reward, with the emphasis on: "Climb your own ladder, one step at a time."

Recognize the Need for Quality People

The company's management team not only provides support to Mary Kay, but also manages the activities of the company's beauty consultants who work as independent agents with their own entrepreneurial focus. She has marshalled a team of sophisticated executives who collectively provide technical support for an army of entrepreneurs, her beauty consultants, the first one of which is Mary Kay.

At Mary Kay, the entrepreneurial spirit is encouraged throughout the organization, with each consultant encouraged to establish her own goals, in keeping with Mary Kay's emphasis on self-competition. The consultants receive training in a variety of areas with workshops covering a host of sales and management topics sponsored by the company. The emphasis is on self-achievement and on minimizing bureaucracy. Although the number of people representing Mary Kay Cosmetics exceeds 180,000, making it one of the largest U.S. companies, the emphasis is on small groups of people, beginning with the in-home sales parties, which are limited to six invitees. This encourages a personalized approach and follow-up that is critical in any business.

Recognizing the importance of balancing the entrepreneurial spirit with managerial necessity—and creating an operating environment that encourages hundreds of thousands of consultants to satisfy their individual entrepreneurial drives—Mary Kay promotes seven core people precepts under the umbrella of "The Golden Rule of Management," which are summarized below and are fully set forth in her book *Mary Kay on People Management,* published in 1984 by Warner Books. (Subsequent references to this source are abbreviated *OPM.*) This is the management philosophy that turned Mary Kay Ash's storefront cosmetics business into a multi-million-dollar corporation in just twenty years. Based on the Golden Rule, it encourages managers to treat staff, customers, suppliers, and everyone else with whom they come into contact with the same care, consideration, and concern they would like to receive themselves. It has brought spectacular success to Mary Kay.

Recognize the Value of People. "People are your company's number one asset. When you treat them as you would like to be treated yourself, everyone benefits."

Praise Your People to Success. "Recognition is the most powerful of all motivators. Even criticism can build confidence when it's "sandwiched" between layers of praise."

Tear Down the Ivory Tower. "Keep all doors open. Be accessible to everyone. Remember that every good manager is a good listener. (You can't learn anything with your mouth open.)"

Be a Risk-Taker. "Don't be afraid. Encourage your people to take risks, too, and allow room for error."

Create a Stress-Free Workplace. "By eliminating stress factors, fear of the boss, unreasonable deadlines, and others, you can increase and inspire productivity."

Develop and Promote People From Within. "Upward mobility for employees in your company builds loyalty. People give you their best when they know they'll be rewarded."

Keep Business in the Proper Place. "At Mary Kay Cosmetics, the order of priorities is faith, family and career. The real key to success is creating an environment where people are encouraged to balance the many aspects of their lives."

In summary, Mary Kay Cosmetics has a people philosophy which acknowledges the needs of its people, their priorities and desires. It encourages self-esteem and self-confidence by creating an environment where the "You can do it" slogan is a reality and personal achievement is publicly recognized and rewarded. It is a company that began with the recognition that the entrepreneurial spirit coexists with the managerial requirements of control. At Mary Kay, management encourages free-spirited, visionary thinking by providing constructive and timely support to its legions of independent agents. It appears that the transition caused by introducing required management talent that plagues many entrepreneurial enterprises was not a problem at Mary Kay, but, in fact, a welcomed and encouraged experience. The self-serving, nonproductive bureaucracy that has stifled many entrepreneurial companies was not allowed to gain a foothold at Mary Kay Cosmetics.

To Mary Kay, selecting the proper people is just as important as displaying the proper attitude toward her people. She emphasizes the importance of establishing priorities; God, family, and career. She appreciates that not all managers recognize this order, and explains that, "Realistically, a woman's priority is her faith and family, and by encouraging this as a company, God provides time for the career. I don't know how it works, but it does. We have seen it time and time again." By recognizing and living this philosophy, Mary Kay attracts the type of women she wants. "It's a way of life, and, more important than selling cosmetics, we are teaching people how to live and get their lives in order. If their priorities are out of order, they suffer and we suffer from their performance. We teach them to live positively in a negative world, just look at the headlines." She emphasizes the importance of "put on a happy face" and even if you're down, "fake it 'till you make it." "I would never let my staff know I was less than enthusiastic, because their spirit depends on my attitude." There is a genuine relationship between Mary Kay and her people. A loyalty of love clearly exists. She feels that part of this loyalty is based on the recognition by her beauty consultants that Mary Kay's dream company, based on her experience in the work force, gives them an opportunity they could not otherwise have. "I give them a philosophy, a way of living positively, to be enthusiastic, to know that life is worth living and it is free. I think they also look upon me as a mother and someone whom they can count on to help them and they know it!" What is important here is that Mary Kay has the ability to understand peoples' inner needs and she satisfies them, because these are also her needs. She is sensitive, compassionate, aware, and she provides for her "Mary Kay family."

Opportunistic

This trait in May Kay is best illustrated by how she responded to the fashion industry's introduction of color analysis for women. It also shows how a negative stroke of luck or problem can be converted into an opportunity.

Color analysis is a process by which a woman's natural skin tone is matched with select clothing colors and cosmetic shades. Although the process was developed to improve appearance, it also limited cosmetics selection and had a negative effect on cosmetics sales. Mary Kay immediately had her scientists review the process and found that she could overcome the limiting aspects of color analysis. After five years of extensive research, Mary Kay expanded the color analysis process by substantially increasing the cosmetics options for women with the introduction of the Mary Kay Color Wheel, which enables a woman to select a wider range of clothing colors by changing her cosmetic colors to complement her natural skin tone. In the end, Mary Kay's approach to the problem actually expanded the refined woman's clothing color selections using her cosmetics as the primary focus.

Motivation and Integrity

While interviewing Mary Kay, we were struck by the fact that she is the corporate symbol, its heroine: her face, her presence, her grace, her signature, and her color are evident every where. The shade of pink applied by General Motors to the Buicks and Cadillacs awarded personally by Mary Kay to outstanding performers has been officially named "Mary Kay Pink." It is the only color in G.M.'s paint spectrum named after a personality.

In *Corporate Cultures,* Terrence Deal and Allan Kennedy accurately point out that corporate heroism is a leadership component that is all but lost in corporate America. "Values are the soul of the corporate culture and heroes personify those values and epitomize the strength of the organization; they are pivotal points in a strong culture. The hero is the great motivator, the magician, the person everyone will count on when things are tough. They have unabashed character and style. They show that the ideal of success lies within human capacity. Since the 1920's, the corporate world has been powered by managers who are rationalists, who do strategic planning, write memos, and devise flow charts. But we are not talking about good "scientific" managers here. Managers run institutions; heroes create them." Mary Kay is truly the heroine at her company.

As the company's symbol, May Kay finds herself under constant facial scrutiny, often to the point of rudeness. How often do employees or customers personally inspect Iacocca's own Chrysler or Victor Kiam's personal Remington razor? Probably never! But Mary Kay's face and her use of the company's products are under constant inspection. She is the personification of the company and without directly selling a single product she is personally responsible for the most sales.

Mary Kay motivates her army of beauty consultants in three ways: through personal inspiration, through an elaborate awards and recognition program and through cross-territorial selling. She inspires through her personal story of hardship and success and through her personal involvement in her employees' work. She monitors the individual performance of her beauty consultants and when she notices a major slide in performance of one, she will personally contact the consultant out of genuine concern for her personal welfare. "When performance slides, it's a symptom, not the problem. I usually find that something is wrong in their personal lives, a divorce, a death, or some tragedy, and I try to be encouraging and a friend and they know I care."

The second way Mary Kay motivates is through the awards and recognition program. As we have discussed in Chapter 1, a key entrepreneurial ingredient is recognition. Understanding this, Mary Kay promotes company-wide recognition through the awards programs. As mentioned earlier, the programs do not promote first, second, and third place, instead they promote the concept that everyone's a winner based on his or her own level of aspiration. One of the first awards a consultant can win is a blouse pin of a gold ladder. As the person's performance improves, a diamond is placed on the next higher rung, signifying a higher achievement level. If performance slips, the diamond is moved down the ladder. It is a public display of a person's achievement in reaching her individual goals.

As the individual continues to progress, increasingly elaborate gifts are given, including the coveted "Mary Kay Pink" Cadillac. Like the gold ladder, the Cadillac is replaced or returned, depending on the recipient's continuing performance, thus further inspiring self-motivation.

To encourage consultants to thoroughly cover their territory and recruit new consultants, Mary Kay does not provide its consultants with exclusive territories. This allows for cross selling and strongly encourages each consultant to thoroughly canvass her sales turf or risk the loss of sales to another Mary Kay operative.

In sum, the Mary Kay effort is based on a three-pronged approach consisting of its founder's personal inspiration, an elaborate awards and recognition program, and the promotion of a competitive spirit by encouraging cross-territorial selling.

At Mary Kay Cosmetics, the company is consumer-driven, with product quality a given. (The company backs its products with a 100 percent unconditional money back guarantee.) The company is sales oriented, reflecting Mary Kay's pragmatic recognition that, "If our salespeople don't sell it, we won't have anything to manufacture" (pg. 139 OPM). Without the customer and without the salespeople, "We don't have a job" (pg. 138 OPM). At the annual Dallas Seminar, tens of thousands of the beauty consultants are disbursed throughout the corporate offices and manufacturing operations to team up with their administrative and production counterparts to learn first-hand what is required to administer, manufacture, design, deliver, sell, and follow-up the sale of Mary Kay Cosmetics. This results in an empathic family feeling where understanding and universal pride prevail. "You're not just filling an order, you're helping someone who supports three children to make a living. If you make a mistake in her order, or if she receives defective products, you've created a serious problem for her, and I know that you would not want to do that. It's also important for our staff to know that we must produce a superior product, so that people will come back for more repeat business" (pg. 140 OPM). Mary Kay believes that *everyone* in the company should be sales oriented, irrespective of the person's position or job. "We must support our field people so that their customers will order again and again. Everyone's job supports the sales organization. Not a single major decision is made at Mary Kay Cosmetics without first weighing the consequences to the sales force" (pg. 140 OPM).

Mary Kay is convinced that administrative and staff people learn to lend their full support to the sales force through exposure to the needs and problems of the field staff. Therefore, everyone in a management position attends training classes covering key field activities. "A person working in quality assurance or product design, for instance, will never fully grasp all the ramifications of his or her job without face-to-face exposure to the customer" (pg. 140 OPM).

Mary Kay gives every employee a set of the company's products plus a 50 percent discount on future purchases. The company wants its employees to use the products "with pride," and is very interested in their opinions and encourages employee feedback. "The more we know, the more we can improve things for our consultants."

As Chairwoman, Mary Kay is enthusiastic about the products but is also constantly promoting a philosophy, a way of life, that applies both to the business arena and to one's private life.

In 1985, Mary Kay was elected to the Sales Executive Club's Hall of Fame. The award was coincidently and jointly presented by the Chairman of Avon, a major cosmetics competitor, and the Chairman of Stanley Home Products, her former employer. After the ceremony, an elderly gentleman approached Mary Kay and said, "When I was at Stanley as vice-president of sales, you were an area sales manager, weren't you?'' Mary Kay responded slowly but with conviction, "No, I was not. You may recall that Stanley didn't think I had the talent to be an area sales manager.'' When relating this incident, she smiled at this author and continued, "We are now bigger than Stanley.'' Mary Kay's point is that twenty years ago, a woman in business was expected to walk two paces behind a man and serve coffee. She radiates with enthusiasm as she promotes her belief in and dedication to promoting female achievement at her company. "If one more woman realizes her God-given abilities and lets go of the self-imposed constraints, allowing her to blossom, it's been a successful day.''

An obvious theme at Mary Kay Cosmetics is "integrity'' in product and people. Although the company sells cosmetics, it promotes "image,'' and the consultant's approach and the product quality must be consistently credible. Mary Kay is emphatic about this as she recounts an early but vividly remembered lesson in integrity.

As a child, Mary Kay was accorded one "extravagance'' by her mother: dance lessons. At the time the lessons cost $8.00 a month, which was quite expensive, as the family income was sparse at the time, during the depression.

The dance studio later reduced the price to $6.00 per month, but Mary Kay didn't tell her mother. Instead, she used the $2.00 windfall to buy ice cream and other treats. Several months later, her mother learned of the reduced rate and lovingly said, "Mary Kay, Mother would give you anything in the whole world that she has. You didn't have to do that!'' Mary Kay states, "I was crushed and it's still there. I still feel it. It was the most important lesson I ever learned. That day, I learned that it wasn't worth it to be dishonest, but to have complete integrity''. . .and integrity is obsessively pursued at the company, in its people, in its products, and in all its dealings with customers.

In an era when government interference has been steadily increasing and corporate irresponsibility and executive duplicity have been growing, it is refreshing to see a self-policing company take charge of its own backyard. When Mary Kay scientists discovered the dangers of hexachlorophene, they eliminated it along with all inventories incorporating the drug, well before the USDA banned the ingredient. The expense and the lost profits were of secondary consideration to the integrity of the product. Mary Kay didn't discover the danger and then try to sell off the remaining inventory of the "contaminated" product; she dumped it. She didn't *have* to do this, but it was her pursuit of integrity and her respect of her customers, that motivated this act.

Chapter 3

*Melvyn Bell of
Environmental
Systems
Company*

Melvyn Bell of Environmental Systems Company

"Resourceful in Creating Assets and Reinvesting in America"

*M*elvyn Bell is the Founder, Chairman, and C.E.O. of Environmental Systems Company, referred to as ENSCO. ENSCO is the largest and most advanced chemical treatment company in America. It is primarily involved in the effective disposal of hazardous waste, such as polychlorinated biphenyls. ENSCO's highly technical approach to waste treatment produces various by-products for various commercial uses.

Apart from its four fixed plant treatment facilities, ENSCO has developed the first modular chemical treatment facility that is transportable to various sites to treat local pollutants. This facility can also be built into a company's existing operation on a turn-key basis.

As Melvyn Bell stated, "The exciting part about what we do is that we provide the technological solutions to health problems resulting from hazardous waste pollutants. My primary function is to surround myself with the best brain power possible in order to develop hi-tech and creative solutions to present and future chemical pollution problems. Equally important are our efforts to deal with buried pollutants in landfills that are poisoning our water supply. I am convinced that waste-to-energy is a concept whose time has come. Driven by increasing environmental concerns and rising costs associated with landfills, energy recovery plants are now economically viable even in a depressed energy market.''

"There are approximately 17,000 *known* landfill dump sites in America and by some estimates there are *three* times that many undetected sites which collectively are harboring materials that are decomposing and threatening America's water system. Also, there are a number of hazardous waste materials that are directly dumped into lakes, rivers, and ponds that are causing increasing health problems. Further, PCB's, or polychlorinated biphenyls, are an increasing health hazard.'' ENSCO is capable of destroying and detoxifying these hazardous wastes.

Its two plants in El Dorado, Arkansas, and White Bluff, Tennessee, are the largest and most efficient PCB treatment facilities in America. Its incineration process in the Arkansas plant destroys the waste by exposing it to temperatures of 2,000 degrees. During this process, energy is developed and captured by an integrated steam boiler which, in turn, powers ENSCO's own operations. The Tennessee facility provides the largest electrical transformer decommissioning service in existence. This process involves draining PCB-contaminated oils from spent transformers; flushing the transformer case with solvents that are detoxified; and properly disposing of the decontaminated case in a commercial landfill.

Ability to Overcome Obstacles

ENSCO was started in 1972 when Melvyn Bell loaned money to the principals for the initial capitalization of the company. At the time, Bell, an electrical engineer by education, was a real estate developer whose projects included the highly successful Fairfield Bay Resort Communities.

In 1973 the ENSCO principals advised Bell that the company was on the verge of bankruptcy and that they were personally insolvent and unable to repay their loan. "Well, I had two choices: 1) let the loan go bad and write it off, or 2) recover the loan by rebuilding the company; I chose to rebuild it." He faced incredible obstacles, nearly becoming insolvent himself.

Bell had his ENSCO loans converted into equity and proceeded to buy out the other investors. "Although the company had a negative net worth, I bought out the investors so we could get to work and rebuild ENSCO without outside interference." With millions of dollars of debt and creditors hounding the company, Bell began recruiting the best chemical engineers he could find and orchestrating the successful turnaround of Environmental Systems Company.

"I clearly remember that the biggest obstacle was financial survival, while at the same time, I was trying to recruit top people and get more money for the best equipment." While most companies on the brink of financial disaster would reduce spending, Bell knew he had to spend more to get what was needed. He bucked the "low-cost producer trend" and pursued the best equipment and the best people.

At that time, there were a number of unscrupulous people in the chemical waste treatment industry. Bell's life was threatened several times and he was nearly kidnapped once. "It's funny, but those things tell you that you are competing effectively."

Motivating People

Bell's strongest attribute is probably his ability to gather and motivate bright people. "I am surrounded by thirty or forty of the brightest engineers and chemists. They are much smarter than I am, but I see myself as the catalyst to motivate their collective achievements. My thrill is watching them work together and accomplish amazing technical advances in our industry. This has made us the leader."

Although ENSCO is a publicly traded company, 20 percent of the stock is held by the employees. "When I got into ENSCO, I was committed to my people and after ten years of fighting to survive, ENSCO turned the corner in 1981." In 1982 Bell called his seventy-four people together and gave them stock in ENSCO for their contribution and sacrifice.

At the time, the stock was worth approximately $1 million. Today, the stock is worth approximately $50 million. "The people that stuck with me are all millionaires and that is a great feeling: to gather, motivate, and reward your associates."

Bell's manner of rewarding his people has resulted in their collective commitment, as evidenced by ENSCO's tremendous achievement. At ENSCO, it is deeply felt that its people are the company's most valuable asset.

Bell's ability to motivate and get "150 percent from his people" seem to have been developed in his youth. "I was not a great basketball player so I compensated by encouraging my teammates. I hated to lose, so I would do everything to energize the team. As a result, we won all 100 of our games." This represents Bell's entrepreneurial approach to managing people: he guides, directs, orchestrates, and attains results. "I guess I was born with the ability to get more out of people by spiriting them to win and produce."

Vision and Proper Timing

"In the beginning of ENSCO," states Bell, "we were up to our arm pits in alligators because I took over the company when it was going under. I hardly had time for any grey-bearded vision. I was struggling just to make payroll."

However, Melvyn Bell and his friend and associate at ENSCO, Dr. George Combs, saw the potential for ENSCO's incinerator waste treatment approach, a concept ten years ahead of its time.

During incineration, chemical waste is decomposed by the same processs by which it was composed: heat. ENSCO plants apply incredible degrees of heat, to break the chemical waste down to its basic elements. The system's scrubbers capture a valuable by-product, pure calcium chloride. ENSCO produces 500,000-600,000 gallons per month of this by-product, which has numerous industrial applications, such as brine for salting roads and as a fire retardant.

"We had the best people working on our project before it was considered a viable industry." It finally became a viable industry when various state and federal agencies began enforcing pollution control laws. By that time, our technical advancements were in place so we hit the deck running, so to speak, when the government began cracking down on violators."

Melvyn Bell was able to foresee that the sheer economics of pollution would eventually gain a good deal of critical attention. "In America, we generate 150 million metric tons of solid waste and 300 million metric tons of chemical waste annually. This does not include the hundreds of millions of tons of waste that have been disposed of over the years, most of it buried in landfills. This waste is decomposing and leaking into our aquifer, polluting the drinking water, and it must be treated. Although these landfills are polluting our water supply, they represent ENSCO's 'inventory' for future waste treatment."

According to Bell, ENSCO's work in the 1970's, made ENSCO "...technically the best, the most efficient, and the most resourceful because we had a ten-year jump on our competition and we had the best people."

His vision has once again brought ENSCO to the forefront of waste treatment with the recent development of a modular incineration system that can be integrated into a plant's existing operation. It provides turn-key waste control and eliminates the transportation aspect of chemical waste treatment—in many ways the most dangerous part of the process.

Achievement

Bell's philosophy about his life is unique. "You must give more to life than you take and whatever I do must benefit people, that's my reward and that's what it's all about, perpetuating mankind in a healthy and playful fashion." That is why Bell recently bought an amusement park, a golf course, and an exquisite resort with superb golf, tennis, and boating facilities. He states,

"Sure, it must make business sense, but there is every reason that it should be fun." This is another example of our Rare Breed entrepreneur's optimistic and positive attitude, a vital quality.

Melvyn Bell's assessment of his purpose in life is: "To create assets, jobs, and contribute to society and mankind."

Independence and Self-Confidence

Melvyn Bell's sense of independence and self-confidence appear to have developed from the independent work ethic of his parents, the hardships wrought by the depression, and from the self-confidence instilled in him by his parents.

As we discussed in Chapter 1, self-confidence is an important trait for entrepreneurship. Most of Bell's pursuits have focused on financially troubled companies into which he has breathed new life, leaving them solvent and productive. This requires an enormous amount of self-confidence.

"My parents' generation taught me a lot. They endured tremendous sacrifice and hardship. They endured four wars, the great depression, and they were directly responsible for the industrialization of America. I learned the work ethic from my parents." Like many rural families, the Bells had a small farm. Melvyn Bell's father subsidized his farming operations laboring at a glass plant where he worked from age seventeen to age sixty-two. "You know," says Melvyn, "farmers are independent and they work hard. I was expected to carry my load and contribute. I had chores before and after school. The farm life made me appreciate balance, hard work, and self-reliance."

During his preschool years, Bell's mother taught him to read and write. "Sometimes we would work twelve to fourteen hours a day on my studies and when I entered school I was years ahead of my peers." This helped Bell to develop a high degree of self-confidence and self-reliance, which served him throughout his academic and professional careers. He developed a "can do" attitude, which provided the underpinning of all of his subsequent pursuits.

"Independence comes from hard work, there are simply no short cuts and I grew up thinking everyone put in eighty-hour workweeks. That was the way it was. At ENSCO there is no place for an 8-5 person, we work hard and we enjoy it."

Sacrifice

Aside from sacrificing pleasure and time, Bell has had to make personally painful compromises. "My father simply never compromised himself. If he received $2.00 more than he should have gotten from something he sold, he would drive thirty miles to return the $2.00. That's the way I was raised. Unfortunately, in business, you have to compromise for the good of the company and for the betterment of its people. It is painful and sometimes lonely, having to live with some of those decisions."

One important compromise Melvyn Bell made involved raising capital through the stock market an act, albeit necessary, that is generally contrary to his instincts and to the instincts of most entrepreneurs. "It is unfortunate, but you talk about your company one way to an analyst, and you run your company differently. We have gone overboard in this country by letting the money people dictate business practices. You cannot run a business on quarterly statements. Businesses must make practical decisions for the longevity of the company. These are often decisions that take years to pay back and that do affect quarterly performance, but without them, you stagnate."

Bell is expressing a generally felt concern of the entrepreneur. In short, that we have become an economy driven by the narrow vision of stock analysts. Spawned by the combination of hyper-inflation and volatile interest rates during the 1970's, the short-term view of the stock market has caused us to become obsessed with money for its own sake and to ignore and sometimes sacrifice the long-term resources that generate the future reliability and growth of assets, jobs, and vitality. What once was used as a gauge to measure has become a counter-productive obsession. Investment flows have been influenced heavily by high-speed information gathering and reporting of the short-term views of analysts who do not understand the unique characteristics of different industries and can't, so it seems, look further down the road than the end of the quarter.

"Stock analysts cannot appreciate the short-term sacrifices that must be made to clean our heavily polluted environment. That means that the numbers *must* give way to the long-term health and survival of the human race, it's that simple," states Bell.

Bell clearly appreciates life's delicate balance and states, "My purpose is to reinvest in America. I remember a friend who, after visiting our house and complimenting us on our antique collection, said, 'Melvyn, why do you have these things in your home? They are not yours. They are hundreds of years old and you are simply a temporary caretaker. When you die someone else will be the caretaker.' I will never forget that and I no longer yearn for material things. My interests now are to contribute to a healthier place to live and I will be devoting much of my time to the aged. Only in this country do we forget our heritage, which was provided by the older generation."

"God put me here for a reason. Not to just make money, but to reinvest it in social causes to improve the quality of life for all."

Chapter 4

Helen F. Boehm
of The Boehm
Porcelain
Studios

Helen F. Boehm of The Boehm Porcelain Studios

"Perpetual Quest for the Best"

D ear Mrs. Boehm:

I was very pleased to learn through your April 8 letter that you have decided to carry on your husband's outstanding work. The many people all over the world who have admired his art will, I am sure, regard your decision as an outstanding and appropriate tribute to his memory. I want you to know that I greatly appreciate your thoughtfulness in letting me know of your plans for the future.

With my best wishes,

> Sincerely,
> Richard Nixon 4/11/69
> President of the United States

Mrs. Helen Boehm is the Chairman and Co-founder, along with her late husband, artist Edward Boehm, of the world famous Edward Marshall Boehm Company, regarded by many as the creator of some of the finest hard-paste porcelain in the world. Over the years, testimonials to the company's porcelain works have been offered by John Hartill, the former president of the British Pottery Manufacturer's Foundation and managing director of Minton China; Mr. Vincent Andrus, the highly repected curator of the American Wing of the Metropolitan Museum Of Art; and many others. However, Mrs. Boehm remarks that her most cherished compliments have come from the owners of Boehm porcelain. Such as when a young boy, convalescing in a hospital, upon receiving a porcelain bunny from Mrs. Boehm, looked wide-eyed at his mother with surprise and exclaimed, "Look Mommy, I think the bunny wiggled his nose at me." Or, when given a lovely bird, Pope John stated, "Don't get too close, it might fly away." And, when touring the Boehm studios in Malvern, England, Prince Charles lifted a lovely flower and remarked, "Mrs. Boehm, only the fragrance is missing."

One of the best testimonials came from mother nature. As Boehm was unveiling an exquisite peregrine falcon he had created, a *real* falcon was placed next to the Boehm peregrine. When unhooded, the falcon began performing its love dance for the Boehm peregrine.

Background

Mrs. Boehm was born in Brooklyn as Helen Franzolin, the fourth of five children of Pietro and Francesca Franzolin, from Florence and Palermo, Italy, respectively. Like many, the Franzolins entered America through Ellis Island after which Mr. Franzolin took a job as a laborer to support his family. He became a furniture craftsman while Helen's mother managed the household. "There is no doubt but that as the youngest daughter I owe my love and feeling for design to the hours I spent watching my father finish small pieces of furniture in our home. My quest for perfection came from my mother's sewing guidance. I was determined to perfectly gather the ruffles on my first party dress. Mama politely showed me, insisting that I rip out and redo the seams until the dress was expertly finished."

Helen Franzolin grew up in a strong Italian Catholic home. "We had much love and as an Italian daughter, I was constantly chaperoned by my parents or older brothers." During World

War II, Helen and her mother visited her brother while he recovered from pneumonia at the Air Force Convalescent Center in Pawling, New York.

"On one of these visits, I noticed a handsome man with thick black hair and a moustache talking and laughing with the injured soldiers in the rehabilitation center. This was the section of the hospital where the wounded were trained to use their hands again through woodworking, sculpting, leather tooling and other crafts. The striking-looking man had his hands full of wet clay and was showing the men how to mold figures. I had to find out who he was. There was something special about him. I looked around and found no one who could introduce us. Not to be deterred, I took matters into my own hands. I boldly approached the work table and said, 'What's your name?' 'Ed Boehm,' he replied, but he didn't ask my name as I hoped he would.

"He began talking about his work as a member of the special animal husbandry division of the Air Force. He was teaching wounded soldiers the care and feeding of cattle, dogs, and other animals as well as how to prepare them for shows. He told me how animals could make despondent soldiers regain their love for life. In his spare time he experimented with clay sculpting. He was molding a percheron mare and foal while we talked. I watched him with awe, for he worked with such deftness and skill. His hands, busy creating a work of art, were like a surgeon's. I was spellbound, and for one of the few times in my life, also speechless. I instinctively knew I was going to marry this man. The fact that he didn't even know my name was inconsequential."

Three months later, at twenty-four, Helen Franzolin became Mrs. Edward Marshall Boehm, spawning one of the most remarkable husband-wife business teams in America.

Born in 1913 in Baltimore, Maryland, Ed Boehm was abandoned by his father, and his mother died when he was five. Friends of the family enrolled him in the McDonaugh School, which housed boys who had lost their parents. His parentless experience led Ed Boehm to state, "You can only be as good as your inheritance will allow."

At sixteen, Boehm left McDonaugh and eventually enrolled in the University of Maryland. According to Mrs. Boehm, "At night, after working a twelve-hour day at the farm, he attended animal husbandry classes at the university. On Sundays he studied but he also drew and worked on sculpting animal figures in clay. His farm wages (during the depression) barely paid for his education, but he studied animal care with an intensity and passion that made eating regular meals and sleeping very low on his list of priorities. He was obsessed with making enough money and getting ahead to allow himself time to explore the world of art."

Ed Boehm pursued his goal and in 1938, at age twenty-one, he raised and showed a Supreme Grand Champion Guernsey Bull, writing in his diary, "I have won my Nobel Prize." At twenty-one he had achieved what many in the cattle industry devote a lifetime to achieve.

His career at the Longacres Guernsey Farm, which he managed from 1934 to 1942, was interrupted by World War II. In 1944, the farm and its prized Guernsey herd were destroyed by a savage fire. He could not return, so he and his new bride settled in Great Neck, Long Island, where he worked as a veterinarian's assistant.

The following paragraphs which explore the source of Boehm's dedication to the animal world and to art are excerpted from *Edward Marshall Boehm 1913-1969*, by Frank J. Cosentino.

"The rest of the story of Edward Marshall Boehm can be accurately chronicled. It is the first three decades of his life for which biographical information is lacking. Out of his misty background came a renaissance talent, a total craftsman and artist who would direct his being and energies toward nature, each day pursue its elusive beauty, probe its order, and reach into its unfathomable depths.

"Suppose one accepts 'You can only be as good as your inheritance will allow.' What of the development of the talent and direction? What gave this person a great potential and all-consuming drive for excellence and recognition, a determination that humbled and intimidated those around him? What force drove Edward Boehm so inevitably toward nature in daily search of origins and meanings?

"The answers lie in the reluctance of Mr. Boehm to talk about his personal life. In his notes, letters, and writings he avoided personal comments and made no references to early experiences. He wanted to blot out the early years because they were empty and unhappy. He never experienced the love and warmth of family life, the uninhibited expressions of laughter and tears between parents and child, the dependence on parental example and guidance. His was a sterile existence (in youth). He was dependent on his own developing character and wits. Personal relations could not influence his direction. Emotion could not interfere with his desires. In his mind, agressiveness and determination became honed to the competition of his society. To survive in a world he found difficult to accept, he had to be equipped properly. To influence or in some way change that world, he had to set goals and let nothing deter him from them.

"His pent-up love and care found expression in God's 'other world' of nature and her creatures, so much so that to see, study, and understand wasn't enough. He loved God's natural world with a passion that overflowed from him into artistic expression. Thus Edward Boehm's avoidance of people. His most consuming relationships were with his animals. He would often say, 'Animals are reliable, true in their affections, predictable in their action.' His garden, aviaries, and the farm helped isolate him from society, at the same time providing inspiration and a point of reference for his art."

Mr. Cosentino's account reveals that, like many of the other entrepreneurs portrayed in this book, the characteristics leading to Boehm's accomplishments sprung from experience in his youth, a time marked by adversity.

As we conducted our research for this book and while studying the life of Mr. Boehm, one researcher independently and spontaneously commented, "Mr. Edward Marshall Boehm was certainly a rare breed." We dedicate the title of this book, *Rare Breed,* to the Boehms, honoring both his roll as nature's emissary to the art world and Mrs. Boehm's contributions to the entrepreneurial world. In 1969, at age fifty-five, Edward Boehm died, having discovered the art form of hard-paste porcelain, with its complicated and exacting formulas, heat treatment, coloring, and assembly. Through his graciousness he left his legacy to a team of Boehm artisans. Led by Mrs. Helen Boehm, they continue to provide the world with the exquisite Boehm porcelain art.

Optimism and Perseverance to Overcome Obstacles

The research undertaken for this book reveals that entrepreneurs have tremendous capacity for making sacrifices and have the innate ability to persevere through all sorts of hardships. Their tolerance for meeting obstacles seems to be exceptional, as their pursuits drive them beyond normal limits. Helen Boehm's story is one in which the successful conquest of obstacles is an abiding theme. "I think a primary requirement for overcoming obstacles is a positive attitude, to be able to find opportunity in obstacles and to exploit the positive."

When Helen married Edward she was working as a receptionist for a Dr. Gillis, an optometrist. Dr. Gillis found Helen's enthusiasm compelling and he sent her to optometry school. She attended the Mechanical School of Optics in Brooklyn Heights to study optics and eye fashion. Within a year she was one of the very few licensed female opticians in New York. "I felt the same sense of elation on receiving my optician's license, number 495, as when I'd won first prize for the design of my junior high graduation dress. Those were two occasions in my early life when the sweet taste of self-recognition was mine to enjoy."

Helen worked with Dr. Gillis, providing the food and rent money for the family while Edward pursued his work as a veterinarian's assistant. "I watched Ed come home at night exhausted from his veterinarian duties and then turn to his hardest work, his art, with a passion so intense that I knew this must be his future life's work. We sat down at our little table and talked long into the night about his need to change his career path. I encouraged him to visit museums and to learn more about the craft, and he talked of his dream of eventually opening his studio. Porcelain had never been a recognized American art form, although for centuries the Chinese and Europeans had excelled in it. In order to work in hard-past (high-temperature fired) porcelain, he needed a larger studio and that would require a large sum of money. Since we were struggling just to make ends meet with our two salaries, our dreams just seemed to be elusive fantasies. However, something happened in my career that was going to help Ed in a way neither of us could have predicted."

One evening, Ed asked Helen, "Who is the finest optician in New York?" She replied, "Meyrowitz on Fifth Avenue, I always go there to buy instruments for Dr. Gillis."

At the time Meyrowitz was the leading international optical center and many of the world's greatest opthalmologists went there regularly to purchase instruments. Also, some of the world's leading personalities visited Meyrowitz to purchase their glasses.

Listening intently as Helen recounted Meyrowitz's history, Ed interrupted and said, "Helen, if Meyrowitz is the finest, then why aren't you working there? If you are going to be the best in the business, then I want you working with the nicest people and serving the best clientele. You could grow and learn more about your field there than anywhere else."

Helen Boehm approached a Mr. Cook, the president of Meyrowitz at the time. Before their first meeting was over, Helen Boehm was hired as the firm's first female optician. "I realized I had to sell myself right out of Brooklyn to glamorous Fifth Avenue. It was the beginning of a lifeling career of selling."

Today, with the presence of women in all areas of the

business world, it may not seem like much, but Helen Boehm's becoming one of the first female opticians in New York and the first hired by Meyrowitz, was a remarkable feat.

Mrs. Boehm recounts, "The next five years were a very happy time in my life. My marriage to Ed was obviously the most important thing that would ever happen. He gave me self-confidence and I gave him confidence back. Whenever he felt depressed about how slowly his work was going, I smiled my brightest smile and made him laugh and made him feel we could conquer the world. Half of the time I was kidding myself, too, but in expressing hope and optimism I almost made myself believe it. We needed each other, we delighted in each other's company, and somehow nothing would defeat us."

Optimism contributes to most entrepreneurs' ability to overcome obstacles. When encircled by harsh realities their indefatigable optimism permits them to envision better times in the future. Here we see Mrs. Boehm mustering all her optimism, to encourage Ed, whose artistic pursuits were sometimes discouraged. "Ed kept trying to push the idea of being a full-time artist out of his consciousness because he said it would be 'complete and total economic suicide.' I was the devil's advocate (the optimist) and I kept bringing the dream to the fore, reminding him over and over again that, 'When we do it, this will be your future.' Although we were traveling down two separate highways at the time, Ed with his animals and art and I with my optician's career, we know that the energy we could create as a team, working toward the same goal, was just plain explosive!"

During this period, Ed Boehm studied diligently, visited museums, and continued to experiment with clay mixtures for his porcelains. He also had a rare opportunity to work with Herbert Hazeltine, the great sculptor who created the revered 'Man O' War,' after the famed race horse. "This was a period of great stimulation, elation, and exhaustion for Ed as he would return home from his studies and apprenticeship with Hazeltine." One evening Ed came home, his eyes creased with lines of exhaustion but bright and rich with excitement and he said, "Helen, I've found it! I know how to make the kind of porcelain I need for my sculptures." Ed's hard work and long hours at last were beginning to pay off. He had finally developed the process that would provide him with the kind of hard-paste porcelain he needed to make the kinds of life-like animal sculptures he envisioned from the very beginning.

"If youthful enthusiasm, determination, and the ability to work ten-hour days seven days a week would help assure success, then we would succeed. We were a team: two opposites—a shy artist and his aggressive salesperson wife—but together we made a whole, a dynamic force that simply could not be checked, and we took on the porcelain world that had been dominated by English, European, and Asian ceramicists. *It was our turn!*"

Opportunistic as to Luck and Timing

The $500 in initial capital that launched the Boehm's came from the veterinarian for whom Ed Boehm worked. However, Ed's first creation, entitled "Champions on Parade," didn't sell, and the veterinarian wanted his money back. "Ed was deeply discouraged and I knew that I must be confident for both of us and tenacious as well."

During her years at Meyrowitz, Helen had developed her own clientele. One particular well dressed, well heeled, and compassionate male customer, often asked about Ed's work. On his next visit, which occurred right after their original investor backed out, Helen, realizing she might be fired, collected herself and gave her best sales pitch to the client, encouraging him to invest in Boehm. He did! In the fall of 1949 the investor sent the first $1,000 of his $10,000 commitment; a considerable sum at the time. With these funds, the Boehm's moved to Trenton, New Jersey, and set up Ed's dream studio while Helen commuted sixty miles to her job at Meyrowitz.

On her lunch hours in New York, Helen took samples of Ed Boehm's work to the fashionable New York outlets. "When we started, people told me it would take a 100 years for Ed Boehm to be recognized. Porcelain had been monopolized by Asia and Europe and I simply didn't have 100 years, I had ten years." Helen Boehm was wearing out shoes during her lunch hour treks, as she would make up to ten calls to potential buyers. "If you are going to collapse 100 years to ten then you simply work ten times harder!"

Her mind constantly racing to devise ways to bring her husband's work to the public, she remembered her husband's dictum, "go with the best," and therewith dropped a nickel into the pay phone and called the Metropolitan Museum of Art. Expecting a secretary or a receptionist, she asked to speak to Mr. Andrus, the internationally famous curator of the American Wing of the Met. The voice on the other side said, "This is Mr. Andrus!" The rest tumbled out in a rush. "I'm Helen Boehm, the wife of Ed Boehm. My husband is the only maker of hard-paste porcelain in America and we would like you to see the handsome 'Percheron Stallion' and 'Hereford Bull' he's created in our Trenton Studio." After a long delay, Mr. Andrus replied in a self-assured voice, "Mrs. Boehm, we don't make hard-paste porcelain in America." Helen, now composed and confident replied, "May I show you please? I think you will be very surprised and amazed at my husband's accomplishments."

Mr. Andrus arrived at Helen's small display shop, which was open only during lunch hours; amazed he exclaimed, "Mrs. Boehm, these are exquisite," and bought the two pieces. Her idea worked! And though quite prepared to give the two pieces to the Met in order for Boehm porcelain to be associated with "the best"; she instead succeeded in getting the pieces placed in the Met earning $60 in the process.

Mrs. Boehm recounts, "Can you believe it, the luck of it all when Mr. Andrus answered the telephone. If he hadn't, I may not have ever sold him those pieces." Luck and timing are critical, but what is vital is to recognize the opportunity when it presents itself and exploit it. Helen contacted the New York Times, which assigned the late Sandra Knox, its leading art critic, to the story. On January 20, 1950, the following appeared in the Times, "Mr. Boehm is a farmer-turned-artist and according to the Met's curator of the Western Wing, Mr. Andrus, Boehm realistic ceramics are equal to the finest of superior English work."

With the prestigious endorsements of the Metropolitan Museum of Art and the *New York Times,* the reception for Boehm porcelain among important collectors and buyers would follow quickly. By 1956, Mrs. Boehm's high powered yet discrete promotional campaign, using newspapers and testimonials, catapulted Boehm art to the point where demand exceeded supply.

Mrs. Boehm's instincts for capitalizing on luck and timing became even more important after Mr. Boehm died. Faced with what many thought was the end of Boehm porcelain, a signal had to be given that Boehm porcelain, despite Ed's unfortunate passing, was alive and well. Harold Coleman, Boehm's attorney and long-time friend, remarked, "Helen, you have always been out in front in the marketplace. You know what the buyers and their customers want. You've always told Ed what to make anyway, ever since he got going in the business." Soon the opportunity came.

President and Mrs. Nixon had long been Boehm fans. As president, Nixon often gave Boehm porcelain to foreign dignitaries. On his 1969 NATO tour President Nixon presented Boehm works to Harold Wilson, Heinrich Luebke, Mariane Rumor, Maurice Cove de Murville, and Pope Paul VI.

Upon his return, Mrs. Boehm offered to donate a collection of Ed's birds to Mr. and Mrs. Nixon. The date selected was August 21, 1969, the day on which Ed Boehm would have been fifty-six years old. To everyone's surprise, President Nixon entered the White House display area where Mrs. Boehm and staff were finishing the exquisite arrangement. Reporters in tow, Mr. Nixon marveled at the beautiful collection.

"I'll never forget the day. One of the reporters asked a question I thought was very pointed (referring to political symbols): 'Are there any hawks or doves in the collection?'

President Nixon laughed and replied, 'Or course not, this is a collection of peaceful and beautiful birds that are favorites of all Americans.' I suddenly had an idea and I injected, 'Mr. President, maybe we should have a new symbol of peace for the world. After all, the dove is somewhat tarnished as a symbol and not all countries recognize it.' The president replied, 'That's a great idea, Mrs. Boehm, you've got the job!' I was astonished to hear the reporters applauding this conversation."

The future of the Edward Marshall Boehm Company would be assured, the signal given.

Helen Boehm instructed her artists to make the 'Birds of Peace.' This lifesize statue whose remarkable detail owes much to Mrs. Boehm's conversations with ornithologists, took hundreds of pounds of clay and thousands of hand-marked feathers and many artists to create. When completed, President Nixon purchased the 'Birds of Peace' and presented it as a gift from the American people to the People's Republic of China on his historic trip in 1972.

The detail was so exacting and the color so real it prompted Mao Tse-tung to reply, "Why would the President of the United States give me stuffed birds?"

Mrs. Boehm recounts, "When President Nixon told me he would be presenting the 'Birds of Peace' to Chairman Mao, I felt tears trickling out of the corners of my eyes as I told him how much this meant to me, to my company, and to everyone who had ever been associated with Boehm. It was a real sign of encouragement we needed after Ed's death. The 'Birds of Peace' made the important and visible statement that the Boehm studio had the talent and know-how to create something that was far beyond what anyone else in the field of porcelain was ever able to do. (Not even the Chinese, to whom it was presented and who founded and dominated the art of fine porcelain for thousands of years, had ever created such a piece.) I felt stronger, both as a woman and as a business person, than I ever had before in my life."

Remarks Mrs. Boehm, "Timing and luck are truly remarkable mysteries in life, they play such a vital role. Only the 'man upstairs' knows why, and you must be resourceful to use it to its fullest. You simply must be alert enough to use the moment.''

Vision and Promotional Skills

During the Eisenhower administration, Helen Boehm developed a solid and lasting relationship with Mr. and Mrs. Eisenhower. She reasoned that, "if the Metropolitan Museum of Art wanted Boehm pieces, why not the White House? After all, the Eisenhowers had many fine beef cattle on their Pennsylvania farm. Wouldn't a gift of a porcelain Hereford bull be unexpected enough to interest them?''

This idea worked and two weeks after offering the beautiful porcelain Hereford bull, Mrs. Eisenhower invited Mrs. Boehm for lunch at the White House. "At one point, the president put his head in the door and I gave him the Hereford bull. His eyes lit up when he saw it and with his famous Eisenhower grin he affectionately patted the flanks of the Boehm porcelain bull. I wanted the Franzolins up there, wherever heaven is, to know that Helen had made it to the White House.''

This relationship with the Eisenhowers developed and grew beyond what came to be a mutual love for porcelain. Frank Cosentino's book, *Edward Marshall Boehm 1913-1969,* which was commissioned by Helen Boehm, was dedicated to the Eisenhowers: "To the President and Mrs. Dwight D. Eisenhower with deep appreciation for their encouragement,'' signed Mrs. E.M. Boehm.

"I learned at an early age that you don't sniff at a target of opportunity. You not only seize it, you jump on it and ride it right through the home stretch. Ed and I have lived by our wits as well as by his talent and my sales effort. Wits and targets of opportunity are closely allied in life.''

In 1957, it was announced that Queen Elizabeth and Prince Phillip would be making their first trip to the States since their marriage. Mrs. Boehm saw the opportunity and her promotional instincts came quickly into play. "Knowing the Eisenhowers would present a lovely gift, I also knew that Prince Phillip was an avid polo player. So, I proposed the idea to Mrs. Eisenhower for a porcelain polo player and pony as a gift and they commissioned Ed Boehm to sculpt the 'Polo Player,' our first of many gifts of State. The recognition we had slaved for was finally at hand. It would mean national, no, international recognition."

Mrs. Boehm's efforts resulted in front page coverage in the New York Times. "Two days later I took the one remaining 'Polo Player' to the 'Today Show' where I was interviewed by David Garroway. The Boehm story was beamed to millions of Americans."

Throughout, Mrs. Boehm's promotional instincts have been both tasteful, understated and unassuming. With this approach, she has established business and personal relationships with kings, queens, princes, princesses, presidents, and heads of state. "You know, when you are the best and when you create the best, yell it to the top of the world. What we create is credibility and honesty in our porcelain art and nobody can touch us, nobody!"

Helen Boehm's promotional talent has borne much fruit. Along with marketing porcelain, she affectively carried her promotional zeal into standard-bred horse racing and polo, where the team she sponsors reached the top as the Boehm Polo Team, winning the most coveted awards.

Her abilities and the honesty of Boehm porcelain even gained her access to the "male only" business world and society of Saudia Arabia. She was the first U.S. business woman to be invited to the People's Republic of China. Her association with Prince Charles is widely known and reported. Boehm porcelain is found in over 119 museums, universities, palaces, and other prominent places, including the Vatican.

In 1986, she geared Boehm up for one of its most exciting challenges, to create porcelain human figurines. Although many have tried this exacting work, it is believed that the Boehm collection will be the most lifelike, with each piece featuring exquisite attention to facial features and the vivid depiction of human energy.

Recently, the Boehm artisans finished two California condors. Mrs. Boehm kept one for her collection and the other was auctioned for $75,000. Some believe the piece is worth over $1,000,000. The statistics for creating this work boggle the mind:

Weight of one wing mold	1,145 pounds
Water for one wing mold	48 gallons
Plaster for one wing mold	665 pounds
Total weight of all molds	6,468 pounds
Total water for all molds	176 gallons
Number of model parts	49 model parts
Number of feather markings	72,000 by hand
Time to produce	3 years
Wing span	6½ feet

Half of the purchase price for the porcelain condor was donated by Mrs. Boehm to the San Diego Zoo for its efforts to capture and rebuild this endangered species.

During the auction, Boehm also sold the proofs of her new 'Little People' figurines. The winning bid was $10,500, with the proceeds going to the Peace Corps Partnership Program for a small children's hospital in a remote part of Africa, where the nearest hospital is 100 to 200 miles away.

These are just a few examples of Mrs. Boehm's charitable style and flair for promotion. As Mr. Boehm told us, "One should give to life more than he takes from it."

Sacrifice and Energy   The Rare Breed entrepreneur has an incredible capacity for sacrifice and the enormous energy required to pay the sometimes painful but necessary price for making his company's existence the number one priority in his life. Without question, all the people we interviewed had made major personal sacrifices.

For Mrs. Helen Boehm the most significant sacrifice was her family. "Many times I would be on the road nine months of the year, pushing Boehm art, and it was common for me to make ten calls a day on various buyers and stores. I remember one Christmas Eve, flying in a DC-3 over the snowcapped mountains of Colorado. It was beautiful but my heart sank as I saw the little lights of the farm houses and I knew families were together for Christmas cheer."

Probably her greatest personal sacrifice was not having her own children. Helen Boehm was raised in a family of seven, in which the family ties were strong. Not to have children of her own was a sacrifice of immense proportion. "At one time we thought about adopting a young girl. We had her at the house on weekends. One weekend, I had to host an out of town buyer for dinner. I left Gloria for three hours with Ed, to return to find her crying for me. Gloria also had relatives nearby—what if they later wanted her back? I couldn't put us or Gloria through that and my travel schedule would have made it very difficult."

Knowing her limits and the extent of her devotion to Boehm art, which was all-consuming, she opted to become a foster parent to 240 children of all races in Trenton. "I love them and they are taken on field trips, to sports events, to museums, everywhere." When one of Mrs. Boehm's "adopted" children needs something, she is the one who provides it, often anonymously.

Recognition for Competitive Achievement

The entrepreneur is driven to compete and to achieve, however, the gauge of success is not necessarily how he or she fairs against others.

Helen Boehm's, competitive drive has never been directed against another porcelain manufacturer, it has been against time and progress. "When you produce the best, your competition is yourself to explore new horizons. Goebel, the great German ceramic house, recently closed its doors at its Trenton, New Jersey, plant. They wanted to compete against Boehm. Well, you can't have my soul, my pride of achievement, and you can't make Boehm porcelain because we are the standard and we excel beyond."

Mrs. Boehm's competitive spirit has been shown in her breeding and racing of Standard horses. In 1981 she acquired part ownership in a polo team that she renamed the Boehm Team. "I carefully researched polo before my investment and everything I do must promote Boehm first. Polo is a game for royalty, and porcelain is associated with royalty."

In 1983, the Boehm Team, led by the high spirited Mrs. Boehm, won three of the most coveted polo trophies: the Rothman Trophy, won at Windsor Great Park; the Texaco International Trophy, won at Cowdray Park; and the eighty-five-year-old Warwickshire Cup, won at Cirencester. When she won the Warwickshire Cup it was the first time it had traveled to America. Her team later earned polo's highest honor by winning the Queen's Cup at Windsor Park. The trophy was presented to Mrs. Boehm by Queen Elizabeth after the Boehm Team defeated the runners-up, led by the Queen's son, Prince Charles. The Boehm polo team holds the honor of winning the World Cup three times and still holds that prize.

"I have always enjoyed being recognized for my honesty whether it be in my sewing a perfect dress, promoting Boehm exquisite porcelain, or rooting on my Boehm polo team. I don't like to lose and I am a gracious winner."

"I never worked for money, I worked for the recognition that Boehm porcelain was the very best."

Chapter 5

J.B. Hunt of
J.B. Hunt
Transport, Inc.

J.B. Hunt of J.B. Hunt Transport, Inc.

"Be Confident to Buck the Trends"

J.B. Hunt is the founder and chairman of J.B. Hunt Transport, one of the largest irregular route commercial trucking companies in the United States. Founded in 1961, the company makes over 250,000 deliveries each year in forty-eight states. It owns and operates 1,700 late model International tractors and has 3,400 commercial dry haul trailers. The company is the largest U.S. truck purchaser and buys twenty new trucks, valued at $50,000 each, per week. Impressive in size, and profound in its impact on the commercial trucking industry, J.B. Hunt is also one of the most profitable trucking companies in America. It generates 13 percent profit on sales, compared to the industry average of 3 percent. "We employ the best people, we provide the best working environment, we buy the best computers, we provide the best incentives, we buy the best trucks, and we provide the best possible service for the best possible price. This all adds up to the most important thing—we deliver credibility."

Vision

Hunt is extremely perceptive, he has that rare capacity to see commercial potential where others, less astute, would not. J.B. Hunt Transport has its origins in Hunt's days as a truck driver in the late

40's. He worked at a sawmill and sold wood shavings to poultry growers for chicken-house litter. Later, he worked as a driver on a regular route near Stuttgart, Arkansas, America's rice capital. While working in this area, he noticed that rice mills were burning the rice hulls, which were considered a waste product. Believing that the rice hulls could be used as litter by the poultry growers, he obtained a contract to haul-off the rice hulls, which he then sold to the poultry farmers. Therein lies the origin of one of America's largest and most profitable commercial trucking companies.

Since its inception in 1961, the company has grown from three employees with revenues of $100,000 to over 3,000 employees with revenues exceeding $130 million. "There's no real secret to it, you have to provide the best service at competitive prices and support your operation with top people and top equipment."

Resourcefulness

"The key to being resourceful is to fully understand the variables that impact your business and manage them," states Hunt. In the trucking industry, some of the key variables are fuel costs, timely pick-ups and delivery, maintenance, equipment costs, maximizing equipment use, labor costs, and debt costs.

Hunt has developed some very unique and refreshing approaches to managing a business. "A critical issue is to recognize the importance of people. At Hunt, we provide a number of incentives to spirit our people." The company pays office employees considerably more than neighboring companies and some drivers make over $40,000 a year. "I keep a little book of numbers that are important to me. One of the critical numbers is the number of employees relative to our weekly salary. Our employees average over $100 per day. Further, we have numerous incentive programs."

Hunt does not for a moment believe that his 13 percent return on sales is serendipitous, he firmly believes that his company should be this profitable and will readily cite his reasons.

"We give our people a piece of the action. Collectively, if they generate 15 percent return on sales, they get a 10 percent bonus, if they earn 16 percent return on sales, they get a 20 percent bonus, and for every percentage increase, in profit-to-sales, they receive a 10 percent bonus. Years ago, this parking lot was filled with junk cars because our people were poor, now they live better, and the car lot reflects that. We believe in reinvesting in our people."

The company also sponsors employee education. "If they [Hunt employees] take classes and get a "B" average, we pay for the class. A key ingredient of our success is improving the quality of life for our people and that begins with education. When they improve, we get better results. I dropped out of school in the eighth grade because I had to work. If you don't have an education, you must surround yourself with people that do."

"Many of my peers think I am nuts because of the way I groom my people and then encourage them to find other business pursuits outside of the company. My friend, Witt Stephens of Stephens Inc., thinks I am crazy to encourage good people to move on. Well, you must remember that to groom good people to get rich and move on encourages fresh blood and new ideas at Hunt. It's counter to their instincts. You can't allocate the entrepreneurial spirit and then try to rein people in, it won't work. So you expect to grow them up and away, that's my greatest reward."

As we interviewed Mr. Hunt and toured his corporate offices and truck terminal in Lowell, Arkansas, his affection for his people and their affection for him was clearly present. "The first thing I do in the morning is walk through our facilities and greet our Hunt family." It quickly became clear to us that he keeps in touch with his people at every level, on both a personal and business basis.

"If my people have a problem, I want to know about it. If you want to help someone, you help them, you don't expect anything back for it, otherwise you are not helping them, you don't do a fat man any favors by buying him dinner, all you are doing is hurting him. You buy a starving person the dinner because he really appreciates it and needs it more."

Self-Confidence

"When people are bailing out, that's the time to move in. The world is driven by commodities and what goes up must come down and vice versa. You need self-confidence and courage to capitalize on this," states Hunt.

Hunt does not believe, as the majority in his industry do, that the low-cost producers will prevail. "Sure we watch expenses, very carefully. However, the quality of our services is our priority. If you lose your credibility, you're dead. At Hunt, the economics of business is achieved through volume, centralization, and self-reliance." To achieve maximum purchasing power, Hunt buys trucks and parts in volume. "We are the largest purchaser of new trucks and we receive twenty new tractors a week." The company has maintenance terminals in Los Angeles, California; Houston, Texas; Little Rock, Arkansas; Lowell, Arkansas; Elizabeth, New Jersey; and Springfield, Ohio. It plans to open additional terminals in Portland, Oregon; Dallas, Texas; Atlanta, Georgia; and Chicago, Illinois.

These terminals play a vital role in maintaining the equipment and also provide relaxing facilities for the drivers. Each terminal is fully equipped, carrying more spare parts than any parts shop in America. Further, by purchasing a single tractor model, the parts inventory is efficiently maintained and repairs are standardized. The company is self-sufficient, providing all required maintenance for its trucks. "We even clean and flush the air cleaner, which enables us to use it three times while others throw them away." Hunt's terminals are capable of completely rebuilding a tractor. Their maintenance schedule is such that, after two years, a used Hunt tractor can be sold with a 50,000 mile warranty. "While our trucker is having his shower at our terminal, his truck is having its bath. We want them both to be happy and clean because they are the Hunt team. That's another reason for standardized trucks, the drivers are accustomed to the same working environment. This improves their confidence and comfort and it improves safety and efficiency.''

While many truckers use excess speed to increase their income, Hunt wants his drivers to stay at 55 m.p.h. It not only improves safety and reduces truck wear, it minimizes fuel costs. ''There is more to it than simply getting the load to its destination; it must be delivered safely, with emphasis on driver and equipment stress. That pays dividends.''

Hunt has aligned the company with the highway police service in the forty-eight states. Where many might view the highway patrol as an adversary, Hunt has built a solid relationship. ''Those people are my eyes and ears. If my drivers are out of line then I want to know about it, and they tell me.''

To motivate and coordinate truck traffic, Hunt has a large IBM System 38. Each truck terminal is linked to the others by computer, enabling the company to receive and process 14,000 telephone delivery orders each day, which are computer assigned to his trucks to efficiently coordinate the Hunt fleet and reduce costly ''dead heading'' (i.e., non-load trips).

Banking, A New Hunt Challenge

Hunt's versatility and self-confidence, have more recently been applied to the banking industry. The industry is currently depressed and Hunt is vigorously pursuing it. ''Trends provide opportunity, so we are going after the banking industry. It is commodity related. In the case of banks, government regulation has encouraged the industry to be lulled and, frankly, most bankers are not businessmen. Deregulation has changed the game to where a business approach is mandatory.''

In 1985, J.B. Hunt purchased the First National Bank of Fayetteville from Worthen Bank. At the time, the bank had a profit of $1 million per year. One year later, under Hunt's stewardship, the bank had a $4 million profit. ''The thing about regulation is that the bankers had blinders on. When the government began to deregulate the industry, the bankers still had blinders." When Hunt bought the bank and subsequently purchased four more banks, he applied his no-nonsense approach. He drastically cut non-banking expenses. "We had banks paying thousands of dollars to various civic organizations they had no business supporting to the extent they were. They had forgotten their purpose long ago. You contribute to a community by building assets and jobs, not by subsidizing the Chamber of Commerce." Hunt streamlined the banks and immediately introduced the incentive program we described above. If the bank makes a 15 percent return on sales, the employees receive a 10 percent bonus. For every 1 percent increase in profit-to-sales, they receive an additional 10 percent bonus. The result was a 400 percent increase in profits in one year.

Opportunistic as to Luck and Timing

The importance of timing cannot be overstated. Knowing when to move and capitalize on an opportunity is a capacity that J.B. Hunt uses with uncanny facility. "We live in a commodity world, which means that prices and therefore, opportunity, are in a constant state of change. Basically, I am a trader who capitalizes on these changes." This trader-like approach is applied to most of his ventures, including his purchase of five banks. "I don't believe that most bankers really appreciate the dynamics or the commodity nature of their business. Money is a volatile commodity, reflected by interest rates. Appreciating the business aspect of banks, we turned our banks around in one year." Hunt believes that the first bank he bought for $22 million in 1985 is now worth $40 million. "Just as we deal with volume and efficiency in the trucking business, we run our banks the same way. I look for deals nobody else wants."

Independence

Hunt's independence was of critical importance when the government began deregulating the transportation industry. "You know, the government never really deregulated the industry, it's still heavily regulated. What it did was to provide 'ease of entry' to encourage competition. At the time, we were well positioned in terms of our locations, equipment, and personnel." Where other companies diversify their sources of supply, encouraging competitive pricing and avoiding the risks associated with dealing with one supplier, Hunt purchases all his tractors from International Harvester (now Navistar) and his trailers from Lufkin. By volume purchasing, he enjoys competitive pricing and, more importantly, he fosters efficiency by purchasing standardized equipment. Hunt also earned the loyalty of Harvester by purchasing 277 trucks in 1983, when Harvester was on the brink of bankruptcy. Also in 1983 he purchased 1,000 trailers from Lufkin, which was also experiencing financial difficulties.

Hunt's self-confidence and independence—vital entrepreneurial qualities—have shaped his career. He dropped out of school during the Great Depression; worked 18-hour days hauling lumber; exploited an opportunity to collect and sell rice hulls for poultry litter; started what has become one of the most profitable commercial trucking companies in the U.S.; and now is successfully re-directing the efforts of his recently acquired banks. A true Rare Breed entrepreneur.

Chapter 6

*Paul Klipsch
of Klipsch
Loudspeaker
Systems*

Paul Klipsch
of Klipsch
Loudspeaker
Systems

"Don't Compete Against Others, Compete for Progress"

While the Japanese have dominated the stereo component industry for two decades, Klipsch Loudspeaker Systems of which Paul Klipsch is Founder, exports 30 percent of its speakers, many of which go to Japan. A large number of Japanese component manufacturers, in fact, use Klipsch speakers to test their own equipment. Considered one of the finest and most efficient speakers in the world, Klipsch speakers range in price from $500 to $3,000 a pair, and some experts contend their performance surpasses speakers costing $25,000 a pair.

Stereo Review, in its July 1986 issue reporting on a test conducted by Hirsch and Houck of the $1,100 a pair Klipsch Forte speaker, commented, "The room response of the Klipsch was one of the widest and smoothest we have ever measured. We cannot pass it off as just another speaker. For one thing, it sounded better than it measured and our measurements showed we were hearing more accurate high-end response then we have heard from most speakers. In absolute terms, the Klipsch Forte speaker would be hard to match, let alone surpass." And according to Paul Klipsch, "Because of their innovative design and the highest standards of construction, Klipsch loudspeakers are simply the finest you can buy, anywhere!"

Background

Paul Klipsch is the Founder and President of Klipsch and Associates Inc., established 1948 in Hope, Arkansas. Born in Indiana in 1903, Klipsch had an obsession with wanting to know "how things worked." It was a compelling drive that, as a teenager, led him to build his first radio a year before the first public broadcast was made. In 1919 he made his first loudspeaker and according to Klipsch, "They sounded like hell, but I was obsessed with the idea of making a clean and honest speaker." That statement underscores the philosophy that resulted in the development of what is now considered one of the finest speakers produced.

After graduating with an engineering degree from New Mexico A&M, Mr. Klipsch worked as a test engineer for General Electric. His love for railroads caused him to move to Chile, where he was responsible for maintaining a corporate railroad system. While in Chile, he pursued his fascination with radios, building a system to receive U.S. radio signals beamed to Admiral Byrd's South Pole expedition. Returning to America during the depression he worked his way through Stanford University's engineering school, earning a master's in electrical engineering. In 1938, he built his first commercial speaker—known as the Klipschorn—and pursued his quest for the perfect loud speaker. In 1941, he published his first of a series of papers on speaker design in the *Journal of the Acoustical Society of America.*

Opportunistic as to Luck and Timing

Klipsch's pursuit of the perfect speaker was temporarily interrupted by World War II. He served as a colonel at the Army's Munitions Proving Ground in Hope, Arkansas. A long-time marksman, Klipsch developed and patented two accuracy devices for small-bore weapons and patented a method for securing the rotating ring on artillery shells to provide for more accurate targeting.

Ever opportunistic, after the war ended, he purchased

some of the buildings at the munitions proving ground at rock bottom prices from the military and began in ernest his research to find the "perfect speaker" while his wife, Belle, worked as a school teacher. Although Klipsch stated that, "Research means you don't really know where you are going," he seemed to know exactly where he wanted to go. The choice of Hope, Arkansas, by the way, as the site of his new company, in retrospect, turned out to be a wise one. The city is centrally located, minimizing shipping expenses. It has a good labor force with a traditional, non-union work ethic and the weather is relatively mild.

Vision

Klipsch was emphatic about his design ideas, strongly believing that top quality radio equipment would achieve optimal performance only when used with equally credible speakers.

Without attempting to delve into the complex mathematics of speaker construction, it is important to explain that Klipsch was focusing on the efficient conversion of the radio input to the speaker relative to the speaker's output. Specifically, if a radio produces thirty watts of power and the speaker can deliver only one watt of sound, twenty-nine watts have been lost in the process. What Klipsch pursued and achieved was the increase of speaker output through improved efficiency of the cone that vibrates and produces the sound. Where most cones vibrate by as much as 3/4 of an inch to produce a sound, Klipsch speaker cones travel less than 1/32 of an inch, resulting in a 20 to 25 percent efficiency rating, or watt conversion, as compared to 1 to 5 percent for most speakers. He also realized that the speaker cabinet does more than simply house the speakers; it is an accoustical chamber, capable of producing certain frequencies and sounds itself. With a series of baffles and different wooden shapes, he created a cabinet that looked like the inner ear. His engineering vision prevailed and in 1948 he sold two speakers. By 1985, he had sold over 18,000 pairs of speakers.

Pursuit of Quality   Klipsch states, "95 percent of speaker
development has been achieved and
my purpose is to discover the remaining 5 percent."

Klipsch's quest for the best, has resulted in the strictest
quality control. It is said that when Klipsch discovered some
speakers that did not meet his rigid quality control test, he put
a match to the load. An audio salesman at a retail outlet comments, "When you buy Klipsch speakers, it's like buying a
McIntosh receiver; you are confident of the quality and the
genius behind the product because the quality control is
throughout." Hand assembled, these speakers are made of
"the finest materials," all of which are U.S. produced. Each
speaker is thoroughly inspected and Paul personally wanders
through the assembly plant and randomly pulls speakers from
crates for further testing, which he personally administers.
"We have the lowest possible return rate. If you do it right
the first time, you make the customer happy and you save
the expense of repairs. We build speakers, we don't run a
repair shop." The speakers are tested in an echo free chamber
specifically designed to capture the speakers' true performance.
This chamber is considered to be one of the largest and most
efficient test facilities in the world.

"Our speakers are matched; one tiny flaw and the pair are
destroyed." Where other speaker manufacturers might discount
or relabel the product with a slight flaw, Klipsch says, "When
my name is on it, it's good." It speaks of pride, quality, and
commitment. For Klipsch, his quest for the best is summed up
by the corporate statement, "A legend in sound," an uncompromising statement that reflects the values of the corporate
culture. Employees and consumers clearly understand the
Klipsch commitment.

The following statement is from a Klipsch brochure and
further reflects Klipsch's obsessive attention to quality: "Our
speakers are built to Klipsch standards, the toughest in the
industry. The Klipschorn is absolutely unmatched for overall
efficiency, frequency response, and freedom from distortion.
No one has ever been able to duplicate the performance of

this superb home entertainment loudspeaker. No other loud-speaker is more carefully built. Requiring over twenty hours of hand construction, each matched pair of Klipschorns is meticulously crafted. No audible frequency is beyond the range of the Klipschorn.''

Ability to Overcome Obstacles

At the time when Paul Klipsch was developing his superb speakers, reflecting "true sound," he met up with an unexpected obstacle: "Consumers were accustomed to traditional speakers and didn't appreciate true sound. They simply had not heard it before."

His awareness that he was an engineer/scientist and not a marketing guru led him to Bill Bul, a major distributor of stereo equipment. A promoter by nature, Bul organized demonstrations of the Klipsch sound at 30 watts, comparing it with a group of highly regarded speakers with a combined output of 500 watts; Klipsch consistently won the sound test. The results of these tests were then used to convince consumers that there truly was a difference, one that was worth paying extra for.

In an era when accumulating debt has become a significant factor in American business and lifestyle, Klipsch has no debt, preferring instead to reinvest earnings. This pay-as-we-go philosophy has a number of important implications. It provides Klipsch with the independence he needs to pursue his quest with minimal interference and allows him to devote all his time to the pursuit of his life's mission, the development of the perfect speaker, by effectively eliminating possible creditor or stockholder interference. Klipsch, in short, prefers to spend his time on input and output ratios of sound and not on price/earnings or debt to equity ratios.

The absense of debt also significantly reduces his costs, making Klipsch a most effective competitor, and adds some financial insulation to cope with contingencies. His need for independence and a strong sense of self-awareness have long made him appreciate the services of a competent business manager.

One unexpected and unwanted reliance debt arose, however, several years ago when Klipsch hired a manager with a blue ribbon management background and provided him stock in the company. The business manager "tried to move too fast and I nearly lost my company. To resolve the issue, I had to borrow money and repurchase the stock at book value which had been sold to him at well below book." Likewise, when his company, employees, and products were threatened by an unfriendly takeover, made possible by the consequent weakening of his balance sheet to buy out the manager, he persevered by incurring additional debt. The debt required to repurchase the stock and prevent the takeover has since been repaid.

Despite this near tragic experience, Klipsch remained confident in his need for professional management, and opportunity struck. After the death of this wife, Belle, in 1976, he married Mrs. Valerie Booles, whose son, Raymond, was a nuclear engineer with an MBA and extensive experience with General Electric. Klipsch hired Richard as the company's chief executive, and the unwanted forays into debt and the problem of management succession were thereupon resolved.

Making The Transition to Professional Management

Most entrepreneurial enterprises mature by way of the founder's ability to recognize the need for managerial talent. An excellent product or service simply does not guarantee long-term success. At some point, professional managers must enter the picture or the company's progress remains limited to the abilities of its founder. The entrepreneur needs a support team of marketing people, treasury talent, personnel, etc. Without this support team, the entrepreneurial enterprise will not reach nor sustain its potential. Much research has been conducted that attempts to identify the point at which additional management is required. Some believe management talent requirements are predicated on specific sales levels, others emphasize the number of people. Whatever the merits of these approaches, our study reveals that the successful entrepreneur recognizes the need for the support team.

When professional management is introduced, entrepreneurial companies will inevitably experience varying degrees of shock resulting from the natural conflict between the free spirited, often informal, entrepreneurial environment and the structured, bureaucratic, and formal managerial approach. These growing pains are understandable and should be expected.

In the beginning, the entrepreneurial enterprise is an informal organization with the founder involved in every aspect of the business: bookkeeping, sales, marketing, and finance. In addition, as we described in Chapter 1, the basic entrepreneurial mentality is possessive in nature and does not effectively distinguish between the founder and the firm, the firm being an extension of the founder. As the organization grows, the entrepreneur finds that a disproportionate amount of time is devoted to nonentrepreneurial activities which are necessary but nonetheless distract from "running the race," which is at the heart and soul of the entrepreneur and his or her primary reason for starting the company in the first place.

As the administrative burdens increase, the entrepreneur will seek relief and introduce the managerial support team. At this point, the *entire* organization will be involved in a structural and cultural transition, enabling the firm to move beyond the founder's managerial limitations and improve the company's ability to achieve its potential. However, like most transitions, there is uncertainty, and morale is often negatively affected.

The conflict arises from the formalization of communications, the introduction of outsiders, and the sharing of power between the founder and management. Where employees once dropped into the founder's office, they now find a communications chain of command. Where the founder was involved in every aspect of the business, some of this presence and authority is now relinquished. Where outside sales representatives once called on the chairman, they now contact the corporate sales manager. It is not uncommon for employee turnover to increase during this transition period because of the inability of some to cope with the necessary changes and corresponding ambiguities.

In the final analysis, the organization should provide structure to the degree necessary, while supporting and encouraging the natural free spirited visionary world of the entrepreneur. The challenge is to blend the founding "family" philosophy and the corporate culture. This equilibrium is critical and the successful transition will result in an organization whose character (ability to overcome obstacles) will be a collective effort with collective rewards. The entire maturing process is a natural phenomena, involving a cultural change during which the founder begins to realize that the organization has a life of its own and optimizes his/her efforts by emphasizing the entrepreneurial spirit, undiluted by administrative constraints.

An excellent example of a company in this transition phase is Apple Computer, Inc., where the co-founder, entrepreneur Steve Jobs, collided with the managerial style of the president, John Scully, whom he brought in from Pepsico. The collision was wrenching for the entire organization. One can only speculate as to the infighting and political alignments that must have disrupted and shook the cultural foundations of the organization.

In such cases—as when the creative visionary ideas proposed by Jobs conflict with the traditional managerial approaches proposed by Scully—there is no real winner. It is suspected that the two personalities represented two diverse extremes and the stock market performance of Apple enhanced Scully's position while diluting and finally eliminating Jobs' influence over the company. One is left to wonder if the stock market knows what is best in the long run, given its propensity for short-term vision. One fact remains; Apple, as successful as it may be financially in the short-term, has lost the vision and creative entrepreneurial style of Steve Jobs, who has founded a new computer company appropriately named Next, Inc.

For Klipsch, this critical transition was made even more difficult by his initial experience with a manager who "stretched his bounds." Despite the difficult, almost catastrophic setback, however, his regard for professional management and his ability to identify good people led to his decision to hire his stepson, Raymond Booles.

Competition and Recognition

"There are hundreds of speaker manufacturers and some are quite good, but my major competition is me, relative to scientific progress." For Paul Klipsch, the process of discovery is the "thrill of it all." His achievements have earned him the recognition of his peers and numerous awards including the coveted and prestigious Audio Engineering Society's Silver Medal.

While many industries are hoping that the government will impose import sanctions to politically subsidize their competition against foreign imports, Klipsch is taking on Japan and the world with his entrepreneurial spirit and his quest for the best. He is not afraid to compete, and, in fact, seems to thrive on it.

Humor

In our world of complications, massive information flow, bureaucracies, and obstacles, a good sense of humor is a great attribute. The ability to laugh at one's self is important, particularly when 80 percent of the world doesn't care about your problems and the other 20 percent are probably glad you have them. With Paul Klipsch, we saw many examples of his refreshing and engaging sense of humor, as in the following humorous line (one of many) during our interview, "I have a photographic memory, but it never developed." He is a true American character.

Upon entering Klipsch's factory one sees a bucket of yellow lapel pins, neatly inscribed with the word "Bullshit." Klipsch explains, "Here at Klipsch, progress is made by cutting through the crap and getting to the facts; not the *possible* facts or the *maybe* facts or the *could be* facts, but the true, hard, *unshakeable* facts."

In church Klipsch takes notes on the services and engages in open discussion with the minister during services. He has been known to walk over the pews to better position himself for dialogue with God's emissary at the pulpit.

Over his desk is a sign that reads, "The Lord Giveth and Uncle Sam Taketh Away."

Chapter 7

*Robert Mondavi
of
Robert Mondavi
Winery*

Robert Mondavi
of
Robert Mondavi
Winery

"The Quality of the Wine Reflects the Quality of the Man"

Robert Mondavi is Founder and present Chairman of Robert Mondavi Winery, and, we might add, the most enthusiastic booster of the company's wines. The winery is situated in the heart of the Napa Valley some forty miles north and a little east of San Francisco. It is recognized as one of the best equipped and most creative wineries in the world. Robert Mondavi is never satisfied with his product; he is constantly experimenting to find better ways of producing better wines. He confesses that he will never be satisfied because there is no final answer or goal, except to produce the very best.

Mondavi's philosophy is very simple and straightforward: to excel in everything he undertakes, whether it is making wine or playing football on his high school team many years ago. His personal philosophy is expressed in his own words: "I always knew that if I worked hard and got into the top 2 percent or 3 percent in whatever group I was in, there would always be room for me."

Mondavi decided during his last year at Stanford University to join the wine business owned and operated by his family. Having developed a basic knowledge of the business by working in his family's cellars, his decision to make it his life's career was based on his belief that Napa Valley wines, under his guidance could become far better than they presently were. The challenge to improve the product, as well as the image of an entire industry, was the prime motivating factor in his life. To the degree that he has been successful even amazes him.

Mondavi admits that he believed Napa Valley wines could become excellent wines, but did not dream they would become equal to the great wines of Europe and become recognized as such. This recognition may yet be nascent in the public's mind, however, the experts, sometimes reluctantly, have succumbed to this notion in recent years. Napa Valley wines have compared well in blind tastings with the best that Europe has to offer. The blind tasting approach, in fact, was undertaken by Mondavi to focus consumer attention on the quality of the wine, not on the label.

Mondavi's chance to run an entire winemaking process came when he convinced his father, in 1943, to purchase the Charles Krug Winery. He believed that the purchase was timely and in the family's best interest. Robert's analysis of the Krug Winery was proved correct. He also recognized at the time that the company faced the challenge of improving the quality and reputation of all Napa Valley wine. Without this, they could not establish an upscale market for their own label. Robert recalls his feelings at the time with the observation, "I knew we could make great wines here, but I also knew we had much to learn and that we had to upgrade our technology." Once again, his sense of the market was proved correct.

Ability to Overcome Obstacles and Sacrifice

The Charles Krug Winery functioned successfully and experimentation for the purpose of improving wine making techniques became integral to company philosophy. Robert's younger brother, Peter, was also involved in the business and didn't agree with many of the things Robert was trying to do. The disagreement came to a head when their father died. The dispute was an honest one over long-term objectives, but the press down-played the serious views of the two brothers and made something of a soap opera of it. The resolution of the problem saw Robert leave the family business with his interest bought out by the firm.

Unfortunately, it took the courts to finally resolve the dispute. As so often happens, a great amount of time lapsed between his leaving and the actual receipt of the money, representing the sale of his interest in the business. Following his departure from the Charles Krug Winery, Robert wasted little time in pursuing his plans for building the kind of winery he had hoped the Krug Winery could be. With borrowed money and outside investors, who held majority interest in the company, Robert had his winery in time for the 1966 crush. Evidence that he was on the right track was not long in coming. In a 1972 blind tasting by twelve California winemakers, Mondavi's 1969 Cabernet Sauvignon placed first.

Inevitably the lack of capital became an obstacle to doing all the things that Robert wanted to do, so an arrangement was made whereby the Rainier Brewing Company bought out the existing outside investors and provided the capital needed for development. In 1978 Robert received his money from his share of the Charles Krug Winery, and he was able, in turn, to buy out the brewing company's interest in his winery. Sharing ownership in the Robert Mondavi Winery is not something Mondavi would ever consider in the future. In other wine ventures he will consider public ownership as a means of raising capital, allowing key employees to share in ownership, but the Robert Mondavi Winery is considered to be "the family business."

Vision

Premium wines selling for $20 and $30 per bottle aren't in the budget for many households no matter how much they appreciate great winemaking. So Robert Mondavi established a separate operation to provide the best product possible for a reasonable price. To do this, he purchased an idle winery of considerable size in the heart of the grape producing area surrounding

Lodi, California. This is the source of a large volume of fresh grapes marketed across the country, and apparently an area that can produce some of the varieties that go into the production of premium wines. This facility now produces about a million cases of "everyday wine" per year. The wines are called "Robert Mondavi Red," "Robert Mondavi White," and "Robert Mondavi Rosé", a personal statement of pride in the quality he has been able to produce at a price that is within the reach of most people. A great many of the techniques developed at the Robert Mondavi Winery are being gradually introduced into this newer operation. This involves a very delicate balancing act, controlling costs to keep the price attractive to the buying public, while simultaneously improving techniques and, therefore, the quality of the product.

At the other end of the spectrum, the joint venture between Robert Mondavi and Baron Philipe de Rothschild brings together two of the most prestigious winemakers, one from the United States and the other Europe, to see what their combined efforts can do to a Cabernet Sauvignon. The first vintage of "Opus One," the name finally settled upon after months of discussion, was brought out in 1979. On June 21, 1981, at the first Napa Valley Wine Auction, the first case produced was bought by a Syracuse, New York, wine merchant, Charles Mana, for $24,000. Not the going price for the regular product, of course, which will be priced in the area of $50 per bottle. But it is indicative of the significance of this unique partnership.

High Energy and Drive

Mondavi says he was blessed with a high energy level, but also admits that having his heart and soul in the business contributes to maintaining his sometimes hectic schedule. In fact, on the day prior to our interview, he had just returned from several weeks of visiting wineries and vineyards in Australia, and was leaving for Europe on the weekend for further promotional work on behalf of the firm.

Self-Confidence

Robert Mondavi denies that he took risks, because he was always confident that he could work himself to the top or near the top in his industry. While the financial risk involved in acquiring the Charle Krug Winery may have been more his father's than his own, Robert's reputation was on the line. If he had been wrong about not only improving the wine quality at Charles Krug, but also that a market existed for the improved product, his reputation and credibility could have been destroyed.

His money, credit, and reputation were at stake when he plunged ahead with the construction of the Robert Mondavi Winery. Even if he was correct in the assessment of his own capabilities, the economics of the operation also had to be correct if he was to maintain his lines of credit and eventually work his way from a minority position to full ownership.

After proving that excellent wines could be produced in the Napa Valley and that a segment of the public was prepared to pay for these wines, Mondavi then tackled the lower end of the market with his "Robert Mondavi Red," "White," and "Rosé" which, as described above, are produced at a winery designed specifically for that purpose. The volume from this facility is about three times that of the Napa Valley winery. The lower priced volume operation could have overshadowed the premium wine business and made it difficult to maintain the premium wine price level, particularly since both operations proudly carry the Mondavi name. This, however, has not happened and is not likely to.

Competitive Spirit

Robert Mondavi's chief competitor is himself. While he has an eye on on what is happening in the industry, he is never satisfied with what he has done and each year tries to produce a better product than the one produced the year before. Since the climate varies every year, there is a new challenge and opportunity. If Mondavi can keep out-achieving himself, he knows he doesn't have to worry about outside competition.

Resourcefulness

The subject of getting the most out of people is one very dear to Mondavi's heart and illustrates his fundamental resourcefulness. His views on the subject can be condensed to something like this: "People must believe that they are a part of the operation, that their views count and that their efforts are recognized. This will result in a quality effort and commitment to producing the best. It is easy to say, but it requires dedication to this principle in order to make it work." These are some of the practices at Robert Mondavi Winery aimed at making his views work:

1) Pay scales run from 10 percent to 20 percent above those of neighboring wineries.

2) Picnics and company sponsored parties are organized to help keep all levels of employees in touch with one another and instill a family spirit.

3) Seminars are held to keep employees apprised of what is happening in the industry and how Robert Mondavi Winery compares with others. This helps instill a sense of pride in the company.

4) Blind tastings are conducted on a regular basis by the employees so they can judge for themselves how their product compares with others. This encourages a family spirit of cooperation, commitment, and pride.

5) Every other year, about fifteen key employees (not always the same ones), are sent to Europe to tour wineries and vineyards so European methods can be observed and comparisons made. In Robert's words, "Things such as this 'reactivate' the people."

6) Each summer the winery is the site of jazz concerts, plays, chamber music, and other cultural events which are always quality performances and are always sold out well in advance. These also help instill a sense of pride in being a part of the operation. The proceeds go to local charities.

Mondavi believes wholeheartedly in the team concept of management. Each member of a team, he feels, is sure to have at least one capability that exceeds similar capabilities in others. The secret, at Mondavi, is to capitalize on each individual's special talent. Robert Mondavi believes that the graduate business schools are not teaching the importance of people to the success of a business. "They (the business schools) and the big public corporations are numbers oriented and they should be people oriented." He realizes that size works against keeping the prevailing culture at the Robert Mondavi Winery intact. As a result, expansion will undoubtedly not come from enlarging the winery, but from acquiring other wineries and having them operate as separate entities where they can carry on or establish their own cultures and even compete with Mondavi. In this way, Mondavi can minimize the bureaucracy that plagues large corporations and encourage the entrepreneurial spirit in all his operations.

In the early going, Mondavi was persuaded that job descriptions were necessary to define lines of authority and responsibility. Once this was done, he soon found that people began to feel "bound in" and were becoming possessive about their turf instead of being open and part of a team. Recognizing that some degree of discipline was necessary, Mondavi has kept the job descriptions, but has softened them with the mandate that common sense and flexibility must prevail. Thus each key employee can work relatively unencumbered while recognizing that he and all the others are working toward a common goal. For Mondavi Winery, individuality, personality, and creativity will not be lost as a result of formal job descriptions.

Achievement

The Mondavi operations are not run without goals in mind, despite the emphasis on flexibility and individuality. Mondavi is the key figure in setting objectives, but he does not dictate. Once a tentative objective is established, all the executives have an opportunity to object, argue, or make suggestions to modify or expand on the objective. Once consensus is reached on what the objective is, Robert leaves it to each individual to do his own thing in his own way as long as he is working with the others toward the common goal. This process encourages contribution and commitment to the corporate goals and recognition for their achievement.

Independence and Control of Destiny

When asked why he made the decision to enter the family wine business, Mondavi replied, "The quality of life was a strong factor in that I could live close to the soil, it created an opportunity to work together as a family, and the challenge was there to express my own individuality and personality in the wines I hoped to produce." As it turned out, the family has worked together, with all three of his children holding key positions in the business. Robert's wife, Margrit Biever, is Director of Special Events, and arranges the summer concerts, the art exhibits on display, and is the hostess for a great many social and business functions held at the winery.

Mondavi had to be independent to pursue his own goals, and it is part of the industry's good fortune that he was. Consumers are equally pleased. Referring to his disagreement with his brother Mondavi states, "As wines have their own character, so do people, and sometimes you must break away and follow your own instincts." His breaking away from the family was a sure indication of this.

Patience and Timing

"The management in big public companies is too preoccupied with quarterly and six-month results and with the 'quick fix' when things seem to be going wrong," remonstrates Mondavi. "They don't understand that people are the most important asset a company has, and it takes time and dedication to establish a culture within a company that will permit the individual to flourish."

Mondavi recognized that patience was required not only to bring gradual improvements to the product, but to have the public recognize this improvement. He states, "Another generation may be required before the general public really believes that Napa Valley wines are equal to the European wines."

Good timing in making business moves is partly luck and partly the result of a thorough understanding of the present state of an industry. Robert Mondavi exhibited considerable foresight back in the early 60's when he was determined to build his own winery. He recalls that big liquor interests were beginning to move into the area and that if he didn't become well established quickly he would be out-financed. However, as it turns out, as major corporations purchased wineries, the quality of the wines often deteriorated since the extended time required to produce premium wines is inherently counter to the pressures of quarterly earnings reports and corporate return on investment criteria in general.

Promotional Skills   Every entrepreneur has had to sell his ideas to others and Robert Mondavi is no exception. The one sale he never had to make however, was selling himself on the idea that he would succeed. When you hear his enthusiasm for what he is doing, you do not question his sincerity. There is nothing of the used car salesman in Robert Mondavi. His beliefs regarding how wine should be sold testify to his sincerity. He believes people should taste before buying, knowing that his product will sell itself, so he is a firm believer in the tasting room approach. The year-round parade of people who tour the winery and end up sampling the winery's products numbers about 300,000. Many become converts.

Promotional activities take up a great deal of Mondavi's time at this stage of his career, and he misses few opportunities to promote both his wines and other wines of the Napa Valley region.

Epilogue The following quotes from a Mondavi pamphlet on the aging of wine in oak barrels gives an indication of the depth of the company's commitment to producing superior wine.

"We are constantly discovering new factors which influence the oak character important to wine during aging. These factors include the origin of the wood (forest, soil, and climate), style of the individual cooper, and traditions of the regions where the barrels are made. By continually tasting and evaluating the wines aged in barrels, we have been able to track the development of each wine and record preferences.

"We decided to take samples of these wines 'on the road' so that amateur enthusiasts and those in the trade can taste the difference imparted by barrels and better understand the contribution oak aging makes to wine.

"The Robert Mondavi Oak Aging Seminar includes six samples of Pinot Noir wine aged in barrels from the Nevers, Limousin, and Alliers forests of France, as well as barrels made of American oak coopered with French techniques. The barrels also show the impact of different levels of 'toasts' on the inside staves, a factor resulting from the intensity and duration of the fire used in bending and marrying the staves. A comparison of characteristics given by new versus older oak barrels is also shown, and the anatomy of the barrel is discussed.

"In addition to experimentation with oak barrels, other experiments are continually in progress on such factors as grape varieties (especially with the 'everyday wines'), stem retention during crushing, yeast strains used in fermentation, filtration processes, temperature control during aging, vineyard irrigation, and so on. This all demonstrates that producing superior wines is indeed an art and not merely a mechanical process of crushing, fermenting, aging, and bottling. I also demonstrate why there will always be differences of opinion when wines are judged by both experts and amateurs. The honesty and integrity put into Robert Mondavi's wines, where cost saving plays a secondary role to quality, will continue to reflect the philosophy of the man.''

Chapter 8

*John L. Morris
of Bass Pro
Shops*

John L. Morris
of Bass Pro
Shops

"Intuition to Satisfy a Need and Visualization to See Its Application for Consumers"

*A*t thirty-six, John Morris is the President and Founder of Bass Pro Shops Inc. Headquartered in Springfield, Missouri, Bass Pro is one of the largest sporting goods merchandisers in the United States and is involved in three different businesses: boat manufacturing, sports catalogue sales, and sports retail sales. Having manufactured more than 100,000 boats, Bass Pro is the largest producer of aluminum bass fishing and pontoon boats. Its catalogue circulates to over two million subscribers, who pay two dollars for the full color mailer. The Bass Pro Springfield retail outlet is under expansion and will exceed 150,000 square feet when completed, making it the largest U.S. sports outlet.

Although the foundation of the company is to provide bass fishermen with a complete assortment of accessories, the "Disneyland-like" retail outlet features fishing, hunting, camping, and marine supplies, along with all kinds of other athletic equipment. The company essentially sells sporting goods, with the emphasis on fishing and marine equipment. John states, "We provide our customers with fun and leisure and we appeal to the 'child' in all of us."

Chapter 8

Intuitive Vision and Promotional Skills   As we stated in Chapter 1, the successful entrepreneur first creates a product or service to satisfy a personal need and then visualizes its application for others who he/she feels have the same need. John Morris epitomizes that approach.

When growing up, John not only enjoyed sports fishing but also participated in competitive tournament fishing, where he was introduced to new equipment, electronics, and baits. These items were often developed or promoted by professional tournament fishermen and were not readily available in the open market. In 1971, John approached his father, the founder of the successful Brown Derby liquor store chain, and requested some store space to sell equipment and baits to fishermen en route to Table Rock Lake, Missouri. This not only satisfied John's own equipment needs, but it also provided other fishermen with "one stop shopping" for their beer and baits.

His father loaned John $10,000 as initial capital to purchase his inventory. With this and a U-Haul truck, John and a friend traveled to Tulsa, Oklahoma, to purchase his beginning inventory. John recounts, "I bought $10,000 of inventory and loaded it in a U-Haul truck and bolted it with a seventy-nine-cent lock, while we enjoyed the town. Just imagine, if somebody broke into that truck, it would have been the end of Bass Pro Shops."

Luck and timing played a major role in the early success of Bass Pro Shops. The year John started his enterprise, Homer Circle, fishing editor for *Sports Afield* magazine, ranked Table Rock Lake as the best in America for bass fishing. John's liquor and bait store was located on one of the main roads to the lake and it received considerable attention and traffic from fishermen eager to fish the lake. Like John, these fishermen usually did not have access to the new equipment and baits, so they began calling him for replacements. This was the inspiration for mail order sales, which eventually led to the now-famous Bass Pro catalogue.

The Catalogue

In 1974 the company bought a 50,000-square-foot former bowling alley to accommodate its expanded retail sales. In that same year, John came up with the idea of the Bass Pro catalogue. His intuition told him that fishermen would appreciate a catalogue that gave them the opportunity to purchase new and exciting fishing equipment that was not readily available in their local areas. Centralized product availability was the idea and John's vision and intuition made it work.

Naisbitt and Aburdene, in their book *Re-Inventing the Corporation,* state that, "Vision gets translated into sales, profit growth, and return on investment, but the numbers come after the vision. In the old-style companies, the numbers are the vision. Belief in vision is a radically new precept in business philosophy. It comes out of intuitive knowing; it says that logic is not everything, that it is not all numbers. The idea is simply that by envisioning the future you want, you can more easily achieve your goals. Usually the source of vision is a leader, a person who possesses a unique combination of skills: the mental power to create a vision and the practical abilty to bring it about. The vision becomes a catalytic force, an organizing principal for everything that the people in the corporation do."

For John Morris, vision and intuition enabled him to see the need for what has become the most successful and widely circulated sports catalogue. He was convinced that other fishermen wanted centralized access to new equipment as much as he did, and he believed that the catalogue approach would meet that need.

To finance his catalogue dream, he approached his suppliers at the 1974 American Fishing and Tackle Manufacturer's Association Convention in Chicago. At the trade show, he promoted the catalogue idea as a cooperative advertising plan, with suppliers paying to advertise their products in the catalogue. Fundamentally, the Bass Pro vendors underwrote the first catalogue, with black and white space selling for $300 a page and color space for $500 a page. The initial circulation was 10,000, and the catalogue sold for $2 to discourage non-enthusiasts from requesting a free catalogue. Today, the Bass Pro catalogue still sells for $2 but now circulates to over two million sports enthusiasts. The catalogue operation is supported by 300 toll-free Watts lines for customer orders and service.

For many professional fishermen the catalogue is considered the "industry bible," providing insight, exposure, and knowledge of new equipment.

The Retail Showroom

John Morris also used his vision and intuition purchasing a former bowling alley for his expanding retail business. The showroom is currently under expansion and will eventually measure over 150,000 square feet, making it the largest sports showcase of sports equipment in the world.

John didn't see just a retail outlet. He visualized a "Disneyland-like" showcase where people could dream, experience, feel, and learn about the products being offered for sale. It is a magnificent achievement where customers can view live bass, trout, and other fish swimming in huge aquariums while viewing numerous sports videos and shopping for unique equipment. For the sportsman, it's a rare opportunity; and, for the novice, an education. Everyone leaves the store enlightened. The experience is exhilarating and appeals to all the senses, as customers can see and touch new equipment and receive hands-on instruction from professionals while watching a nine-pound black bass cruise through one of the aquariums or see a two-pound trout undulating its gills in one of the rock brooks. John Morris' vision and amazing showcase creations actually put the visitor in the fishing environment, making the visit an intimate and personal experience.

As with other people we interviewed, the Bass Pro objectives are clearly stated in the founder's philosophy: "The friendship of the fishermen we serve is the foundation of our progress." This clear and unequivocal statement serves as the rallying point for the 2,000 Bass Pro employees. It is a statement of purpose and acknowledges that the customer is why Bass Pro exists and excels. The goals by which Bass Pro's success is measured are summed up in the corporate policy statement, "We deliver quality, selection, price, and service." These are commitments and they solicit action. These are not numbers without meaning. They lead directly to actions which result in the achievement of the company's financial objectives. For too long, corporate America has been doing it backwards, putting the numbers first and making their achievement an obsession, often resulting in the sacrifice of quality, service, and customer recognition.

Picture yourself as a sales representative at Bass Pro Shops. You are called to the annual meeting and John Morris states the following as Bass Pro's corporate objectives:

> "I expect all of you to actively contribute to a 20 percent return on equity this year with particular attention to our 3:1 debt/equity position, and carefully monitor your section to see that we achieve a 2:1 current ratio. And, remember folks, we must realize a 6 percent return on assets."

Inspiring? Hardly!

There are probably only two people in the audience who can identify with this: the chief financial officer and the comptroller. In most cases, the president of the company rarely understands this talk and at Bass Pro, John Morris would have 2,000 people walking in circles trying to find out which department handles the current ratio. Sound silly? Sure it does, but the vast majority of American companies view life by the numbers. This has been a costly mistake, resulting in the death of many companies and the importation of several industries, which in turn are causing tremendous social and economic stress.

As we trace the origin of this numbers mentality we see two primary sources: stockholders and business schools. As the spawning ground for American business executives, business schools focus considerable attention on the numbers. Likewise, since stockholders must choose from thousands of corporate stock issues, their method of selection is based primarily on return on stockholders' investment within a relatively short period, such as five to seven years. As a result, the fundamentals of quality, service, and customer satisfaction are being sacrificed in favor of the numbers.

Through the board of directors, stockholders put pressure on the CEO and president to achieve certain return on equity objectives. These executives are constantly concerned about analysts' reviews of company performance. The top executives then pass their numbers to their lieutenants who pass them down the line. Ultimately this gets converted into action that far too often results in sacrificing the basis for being in business, as quality, service, and customer recognition are diluted for the NUMBERS. Ultimately, the company's performance reflects its poor quality and service, the almighty numbers begin to reveal it, and the CEO is ousted.

In an age of incredible amounts of information, the CEO, of course, will always be measured by certain numbers. But he/she must have the vision to convert the numbers into corporate objectives that emphasize quality, service, and customer needs. This makes sense mostly because employees can identify with these objective's since they too are customers of other companies themselves and know what they respond to in making their own consumer choices. As Morris aptly states, "At Bass Pro we have the luxury of focusing on the long haul, without concern for stockholder review of quarterly performance. Our country has lost much of its long-term vision because the stockmarket is geared toward short-term and quarterly performance."

The Bass Pro corporate objectives of quality, selection, price, and service are summarized in its catalogue as follows:

Quality—Only the Finest. In this catalogue you will find only the finest quality sporting goods. Top national brands, featuring our exclusive Bass Pro Shops labeled products. Our staff tests each new product to assure every item meets our strict standards and represents solid lasting value.

Selection—Being First With the Products You Want. We are specialists, as bass fishing is our business and not just a sideline. Professionals on our staff regularly visit major fishing tackle plants both in the United States and abroad. We attend trade shows and are present at most major professional tournament competitions. Our buyers work hard to find and/or develop new products with features to meet your changing needs.

Price—We Simply Do Not Like to Be Undersold. To the best of our knowledge, the prices contained in this catalogue are as low or lower than the everyday prices presently offered on the shelves of any retail sporting goods outlet anywhere. You can order from this catalogue with complete confidence that our prices are extremely low. Our low price policy is your insurance that the price is right! You always get our lowest current price.

Service—Convenient Home Delivery With Your Satisfaction Guaranteed! Forget parking problems and crowded stores. Save gas, time, and money by leisurely shopping from the comfort of your own home. We maintain a large inventory and strive to ship most orders within twenty-four to forty-eight hours from the time they are received. We guarantee complete satisfaction or your purchase will be promptly exchanged or money refunded.

The book *In Search of Excellence* emphasizes "Getting Close to the Customer." At Bass Pro Shops, most of the employees, including John Morris, are customers. Unlike many companies, Bass Pro's products are widely used by the staff. Through an internal program called "Tell Us," employees are urged to make suggestions and recommendations concerning the company and its products. These suggestions are followed up at weekly staff meetings and achievement awards are provided. John Morris is extremely close to the customer, and when he's not orchestrating Bass Pro efforts he is in the water using, testing, and competing with its products. He lives the business and fully understands his customers.

Quality, selection, price, and service are the corporate

attributes emphasized by John Morris, and the numbers reflect their significance. Although most CEOs view the stockholders as their primary constituents, John Morris believes the customer is the primary responsibility. It's often said, "If you want to be successful catching fish, you must think like a fish." Bass Pro is consistently successful because its management and employees think like the customer.

Boat Manufacturing   In 1978, Bass Pro introduced its now famous aluminum Bass Tracker fishing boat. By 1985 it had sold over 100,000 boats, making it the largest manufacturer of aluminum fishing and pontoon boats.

Being customer oriented and a fisherman, John consulted his father and uncle, both avid fishermen, to gain their thoughts on the boat idea. The result was the successful design and production of a fully equipped bass boat that sell for $3,995-5,995, as compared to other boats, which sell for $6-8,000. This remarkable price difference was achieved by standardized production and by selling the boats as fully equipped packages.

By standardizing production and offering one model, Bass Pro eliminateed approximately 20 percent of the overhead associated with the costly "make-ready time in manufacturing that is necessary to gear up and change over a production operation," to produce a different model. The Bass Tracker production approach enabled Bass Pro to volume order components at considerable discount, further reducing the cost. Thus the customer receives a high-quality, well-equipped fishing boat for almost half the price of comparable boats.

Today, Tracker Marine offers pontoon boats, duck blind pontoon boats, and a new fiber Kevlar boat. All are sold as a package, including the trailer, and, as described above, still are priced very competitively.

Appreciation for Good People

The Bass Pro story is one of incredible growth in sales, retail space, and employees. This pace has definitely caused stress for John Morris and his employees. As the demand grew, John found himself moving more into the people management area and away from merchandising, his real love. He seems to have gone through the transition stage rather well, and stresses the importance of attracting and motivating good people. "People issues bring me the greatest pleasure or they can rip your heart out."

According to John Morris, the key to keeping good people and maintaining high morale and productivity is flexible and ongoing communications. People need to be heard, and by soliciting their input, John Morris receives timely information and obtains the commitment necessary to achieve corporate goals. When people are provided an avenue for expression and this expression is incorporated in company policies, goals, and objectives, the organization is acknowledging a human need to be recognized. This recognition is converted to commitment and achievement, providing corporate/individual compatibility.

In the many books discussing the new information era and focusing on all types of "excellence," there is scant mention of the creative power of communications. Without an atmosphere that allows everyone to be heard and recognized, there is marginal corporate commitment and therefore marginal achievement. Achievement comes from commitment and commitment comes from recognition, which is spawned by communications and especially by listening. *All* the people we interviewed were intense listeners, but they also have excellent "crap detectors" to filter the central issues from the garbage, and John Morris epitomizes this talent.

Although we have what is considered a free and open society, today's corporate cultures often actually discourage communications. People are not encouraged to freely express themselves, or to challenge, confront, and eventually change circumstances or policies. People need a forum to vent their ideas and they need an opportunity to contribute; anything less is to deny a natural human need and results in employee attitudes of "doing time." The big loser in a closed communications environment is the corporation, because it fails to recognize and take advantage of the incredible information people have, which is not given the chance to percolate and enrich the entire organization.

Successful entrepreneurs are aware of their own need to be recognized and they encourage their people by incorporating open and candid communications as a part of the corporate culture. Through various formal and informal means, John Morris recognizes and encourages people participation. In *Re-Inventing the Corporation,* Naisbitt and Aburdene stress that middle management is being replaced by computer information. The result is to push decision making farther down the line. The magnitude of these decisions will be significantly greater than those previously made by middle managers, because of the volume of information available. This will greatly increase the need for open communications. Organizations with open communications will adapt to change more readily in the "Megatrends" society; companies with closed communications will be in for a shock because management power and information power will collide.

At Bass Pro, attention to people, whether a customer or an employee, is critical, and is Morris' primary concern. He has created a fun business and his people are committed to success because they are recognized and strongly encouraged to be vocal and participate as equals.

Chapter 9

*J.R. (Jack)
Simplot
of J.R. Simplot
Company*

J.R. (Jack) Simplot of J.R. Simplot Company

"Visionary Resourcefulness in Pursuing the Sport and the Chase"

*J*ack Simplot is the Founder and Chairman of the J.R. Simplot Company, an Idaho-based corporation with sales approaching $1.5 billion. This giant, privately held, conglomerate rose from the sandy loam of the mighty Snake River Valley to become the world's largest potato processor, producing in excess of one billion pounds of french fries per year, most of which are sold to McDonalds. The company is one of the largest U.S. cattle operations, feeding over 150,000 head, and owns one of the West's largest phosphate mining and fertilizer manufacturing operations. Jack recently became heavily involved in Micron Technology Inc., a high-tech company which has revolutionized electronic microchips and their manufacturing process.

At age seventy-eight, and after sixty years of business involvement, Jack Simplot is the quintessential entrepreneur. His vitality and taste for business and its challenges haven't diminished one iota. The Simplot story shows us a man possessed with optimism as he bellows, "We finally got rid of all the don'ts and can'ts around here and if we want to spend $100 million on a project, we do it; there is no one saying we can't." Simplot regales as he shares a story about the optimist and the pessimist. "When shown a room full of horse manure, the pessimist will recoil with disgust while the optimist will leap onto the pile and vigorously thrash through it exclaiming, 'Somewhere in here there's a pony!' " For Jack Simplot there have been plenty of rooms full of horse manure and his resourcefulness and tenacity usually have enabled him to come up with the pony. The Simplot saga is also underscored with Jack's pursuit of balance and synergy in his various business efforts and with his absolute respect for efficiency, evidenced by how he uses waste by-products from his various operations the way a diamond cutter scores a precious stone.

Simplot learned the work ethic from his father, who in 1909 left a fertile Iowa farm for the sagebrush of Idaho and a little more than a 160-acre titled homestead overlooking the Snake River. The land was hard and the weather extreme, with biting winters and desert summers; conditions that forged and honed young Jack's mettle. Simplot's father was a driver and a disciplinarian and Jack was expected to produce and contribute to the family. Asked about his secrets of success Simplot replies, "There were no secrets, just hard work, a little luck, tenacity, getting a little capital together to get started, and hanging onto what you build." He recognizes that the challenge to achieve was a driving force, coupled with his immense tenacity in the face of what seemed to be insurmountable financial obstacles. "Many times in those early years I was tempted to sell out just to get out from under the pressure."

Vision and Resourcefulness

Jack left school and his family at fourteen, never finishing the eighth grade. From the beginning, he appreciated efficiency and abhorred waste, a trait learned as a boy while working on the family farm. "We utilized everything and we threw away nothing." This statement forms the foundation for the Simplot empire, which began for Jack when he collected rags for mills. His first business venture was started with $700 he had saved from his rag sales.

In 1927, Simplot was trading horses, cattle, and hogs when the bottom fell out of the hog market. Prices plummeted to a sustained point below the cost of raising the animals. Hog slaughter was rampant, with whole herds being killed and dumped into mass graves. This waste struck a vital and sensitive cord in Simplot, who began gathering hogs. "I got big ones, small ones, skinny ones, and I ended up with 700 pigs at an average cost of one dollar each." He faced his first cash flow problem, with his money gone and no working capital to feed his investment. From this experience he learned the fundamental entrepreneurial skill of capitalizing one's own labor. He also assumed a position opposed to the trend; farmers were rushing to get out of the hog business and Simplot was getting into it. In order to feed his pigs he collected discarded, undersized (culled) potatoes which were considered a waste product by the farmers. He also stalked and killed wild horses, which roamed by the thousands in the Idaho mountains at that time. Stripping the hides and selling them for gas money, he cooked the horse meat with the potatoes and fed the slurry to his hogs.

Simplot's move into the hog business may have seemed a misguided blunder, but that was certainly not the case. He fully realized that the prices of hogs, like all commodities, are volatile; therefore what comes down will eventually go up. One year after Simplot bought his pigs, the hog market turned upward due to the scarce supply resulting from the pig slaughter, and Slimplot sold his $700 investment for $7,800, a sizeable sum of money in 1928. This efficiency and resourcefulness is the common thread throughout Simplot's life, to be repeated in a variety of situations.

Simplot used his $7,800 to lease a farm, buy equipment, a truck, some horses and "my first set of good clothes." He grew potatoes on a portion of the farm he leased. While on one of his many elk hunting trips, Simplot learned of a man who had designed an electric potato sorting machine that allowed culled potatoes to be removed much more efficienctly, eliminating a lot of costly manual labor. Simplot and his landlord bought the sorter for $700.

The potato sorter proved to be so effective that Jack found the time not only to sort his and his landlord's potatoes, but was able to sort potatoes for other farmers. However, like many of Simplot's ventures, it was not without its problems and was to be the first of his many joint ventures that resulted in a parting of the principals.

Simplot's landlord partner felt that custom sorting was benefiting their competitors and a disagreement resulted concerning the sorter's continued use for other potato growers. Simplot's "no waste" philosophy was intolerant to the thought of an idle machine, so he proposed a coin toss to determine both the fate and ownership of the sorter. The coin landed in Simplot's favor and two years later, in 1930, he had potato sorters and warehouses in thirty locations throughout Idaho.

By reviewing the evolution of Simplot's operations we can see a connecting thread—the reuse of waste. For instance, Simplot's potato operation produces large amounts of waste with considerable costs for disposal. After extensive experimentation, Simplot was able to determine that cattle yields improved with potato feed, as compared to grain feed. The company began pulverizing potato waste to make a slurry for the cattle whose pens adjoined his potato processing plants. He then entered into a marketing agreement to sell the cattle to Iowa Beef Processors, the largest U.S. beef processor. Although this arrangement serves as a hedge of sorts against falling cattle prices, it does not insure against all possible losses on all his cattle sales. But, as long as any incurred cattle losses are less than the heavy costs of disposing the potato waste, the cattle operation saves money for the potato operation. At the same time, potato waste is also being converted to ethanol, which, as a gasoline additive, boosts octane ratings. This arrangement exhibits resourcefulness of the highest order.

Simplot's ventures, with few exceptions, have all been somewhat themeatic (but not dogmatic); he has been able to spot, develop and commercialize opportunities that passed most by unnoticed. The efficient utilization of waste and its commercial application has been at the heart of just about all of

Simplot's ventures. In Simplot's second real venture, he collected culled onions from Idaho farmers. He collected the rejected onions for a broker in Berkeley, California, who made onion flakes and powder. When the processor began falling behind in his payments to Simplot, he drove to California to collect the debt. While waiting in the processor's office he met a buyer of the onion powder and flakes, who had traveled to California from Chicago to see why his shipments were late. After waiting quite some time for the processor, Simplot and the buyer went to lunch where they cut a deal. Written on the back of an envelope, the agreement called for Simplot to directly process the culled onions into flakes and powder for delivery to the Chicago buyer. This would also turn out to be Simplot's second ill-fated partnership, as the men initially agreed to put up $25,000 apiece.

As Simplot stated, "There I was with culled onions and a contract scratched on an envelope to sell flakes and powder but I had no equipment or building to do the job." He returned to the processor's office and collected his debt, then followed a truck delivering culled onions to the processing plant. There he saw the machinery required to dehydrate the onions; an old prune dryer manufactured in St. Helena, California, just north of Berkeley. He drove to the manufacturer and ordered the machinery.

Capital for the venture was not an obstacle because of the $25,000 investment by the Chicago buyer. Simplot's $25,000 came from his potato sorting operations. Finally, after several months of searching for a suitable location where the locals would tolerate the onion odor, and investing a total of $85,000, Simplot's plant was operating, but no money had yet been received from the Chicago onion buyer. Simplot explained, "I was damn near broke, but fortunately the plant ran like a top and it netted $50,000 the first month, and guess who sent his half of the venture capital? The Chicago broker! And guess who sent it back? Me! Hell, I had taken all the risk and he put up his money after seeing the operation run successfully." By the end of the first year of operations, he had made several hundred thousand dollars, his first real money, earned in the depths of the Depression.

Virtually every venture Simplot pursued during those years would frighten today's venture capitalists. Buying hogs with no money for feed when the market was severely dissipated and entering into a contract to supply sizeable amounts of onion flakes and powder without knowing or having the means to carry out the terms of the agreement are not the kinds of ventures described in the business plans that reach most venture capitalists desks today. During that time Simplot also bought fourteen foreclosed farms with no money down, which could have been a fiasco. But as a trader he fully appreciated the volatility of land prices. "The key is being on the right side of the market, which is often the opposite side of the trend." As his operations expanded, this attitude never changed, much to the consternation of his business partners and creditors, "the faculty of the school of can'ts and don'ts."

During WWII, a Simplot chemist approached Jack with the idea of freezing french fries. He was skeptical because previous attempts resulted in decomposition when the product thawed. The chemist, working on the dehydration of potatoes for the war effort, convinced Simplot that the water levels could be controlled, thus solving the problem. Seeing the potential of a frozen french fry potato market, he made a substantial investment in the idea and before long the product was ready. After many failed attempts to market the product to McDonalds, Simplot was finally able to convince Ray Kroc, its founder, to use the frozen product in his restaurants. As a result, today Simplot provides a large share of frozen french fried potatoes to McDonalds, worldwide.

In 1980, Simplot turned to yet another challenge; investing in a new computer chip manufacturing company, Micron Technology Incorporated. On the surface, this would seem completely out of sync with Simplot's operations, but closer scrutiny reveals that chips are bought and sold just like commodities. And as we have seen, resources and commodities are Jack Simplot's forté and, therefore, Micron could be viewed as being quite compatible with his basic approach to business.

Micron is a modern high-tech entrepreneurial venture involving some of the nation's most talented and accomplished electrical engineers and technicians. They design and manufacture one of the world's most efficient and cost competitive chips in a plant built at 20 percent of the cost of comparable operations. Although many venture capitalists, bankers, and competitors predicted that the Micron plant would never produce a workable chip, the company produces what some consider the best chip in the world. It has the best fail/safe record of any chip and it's price competes head-to-head with Japanese chips, regardless of the fluctuations in the value of the dollar.

After four years and a $20 million venture capital investment, and despite its numerous skeptics, including various Simplot employees, Micron began producing its revolutionary chip. A complete account of this saga is found in Chapter 11 of George Gilder's book, *The Spirit of Enterprise.*

Why would Simplot pursue or be remotely interested in Micron Technology, with its new risky chip, heavy competition, and basic uncertainty? Because of the challenge these things offered him, and because he admired the tenacious entreprenurial spirit of Joe and Ward Parkinson, Micron's founders. Simplot identified with them, and they allowed him to relive his early, formative entrepreneurial experiences, with all the obstacles, struggles, independence, defiance, and rewards. During our meeting, Simplot opened his hand to reveal the tiny Micron chip and claimed, "With this little chip, we will revolutionize world communications, the most valuable commodity."

More recent examples of Simplot's ability to manage risk include his acquisition of a major California fertilizer and chemical operation during bankruptcy proceedings and the unprofitable frozen vegetable and fruit operations of Dalgety Inc. Simplot also purchased a West German potato processing operation that has lost money for six years and is involved in potato operations in Thailand and Turkey.

Opportunistic as to Luck and Timing

It can be argued that Simplot has enjoyed more than his share of luck. Undoubtedly some measure of luck contributed to his success, but Jack's shrewdness, tenacity, hard work, and solid understanding of agriculture also were major factors. Perceptiveness seems to underly much of what could be seen as Simplot's good fortune. As he states, "God gives you five cards in the game of life; your physical characteristics, your heritage, your country, and two wild cards for you to play."

During World War II, Simplot was developing new applications for his onion dryer and was involved heavily in the potato business. He was awarded large contracts for dehydrated potatoes and vegetables for American troops providing nearly 40 percent of the Army's dried food requirements. As the military's needs expanded and Simplot was able to expand his operations, he ran into another obstacle: the excess profits tax imposed by the IRS, which was diverting money that was needed for reinvestment in capital equipment to meet the military's food requirements. Two government agencies were working against each other and Simplot was in the middle. To resolve this and find the necessary investment capital, he formed numerous partnerships and continued to expand his operations.

After the war, and no longer insulated by the military, the IRS swooped down on Simplot and his various partnerships. The military honored Simplot's contributions with the "Excellence" medal for outstanding industrial performance during the war, while the IRS pursued him relentlessly levying a $2.5 million tax bill and forced the unwinding of his extensive partnerships. Out of this trouble was born the present day J.R. Simplot Company.

Responding to the IRS's mandates, Simplot approached his various business partners and offered them stock in the newly formed company in exchange for their ownership in the partnerships. For the most part, the partners opted for cash, citing a projected recession and the drastic decline in the demand for dehydrated vegetables.

At this point Simplot resourcefully turned his partners' reasoning to his advantage. He offered them cash for their position as they wanted, but at rock bottom prices reflecting their own recession scenarios. He was broke and had a huge IRS tab, but he put enough cash together to buy out all the partners who refused stock in the new J.R. Simplot Company. He was broke and deeply in debt, but he was now the unquestioned owner of his company.

Reflecting on this incident Jack says, "Sure there's been some luck, but timing to capitalize on it is critical. When the time is right you gotta go for it. There are two kinds of people in this world, those that think about it and those who act. And I act!" A sign on Simplot's desk underscores his philosophy: "Nothing will ever be attempted if all possible objections must be first overcome."

Drive and the Energy to Overcome Obstacles

The many obstacles in Jack Simplot's life brought him to the point of physical and mental exhaustion more than once, but these same challenges also enabled him to develop unusual stamina and character. Now at age seventy-eight, he plans to be "around for another ten or twenty years. Oh hell, make it forty years!" One would be cautioned not to bet against this, since on the morning we met, Simplot had skied fifteen miles and the day before had rode his horse ten miles. Over the years, Simplot's drive has been used to overcome several obstacles along the way as the following incidents illustrate.

During the war, fertilizer, like many commodities, became scarce. This threatened the vegetable and potato industry and Simplot's ability to meet the Army's food requirements. Simplot's fertilizer supplier offered to provide the phosphate ingredients if Jack would build his own fertilizer processing plant, which he agreed to do. As the plant neared completion, the supplier informed Simplot that the military draft had created a shortage of miners and he found himself unable to provide the phosphate he had promised. Where others would quit, Simplot's philosophy was "Don't give me a thousand reasons why I can't, just give me one why I can." Simplot and his geologist became prospectors and discovered some of the largest phosphate deposits in the western hemisphere. As a result, today Simplot operates two phosphate mines and five fertilizer manufacturing plants.

The wood needed to build potato crates also became scarce during the war. Jack's answer was to build sawmills. "I built four sawmills to meet my needs and began producing other cuts of wood." If one word can describe Jack Simplot it is "vitality."

Competitiveness

Simplot's competitive spirit has taken many different forms over the years but it becomes especially active when he believes his domain is threatened. Although the Simplot story is one of balance, efficiency, and resourcefulness, on occasion it has also been a story of aggressiveness and combativeness. This side of Simplot was fully revealed in 1976 in what was referred to as the "Potato War."

In September 1975, Simplot noticed that the price of potatoes for May 1976 delivery on the futures exchange was rising disproportionately in relation to normal supply. Acutely aware of seasonal prices and demand, he knew also that significant unusual rises in these prices would mean either his having to pass the additional costs on to his customers or reduce his profit margin. Since neither alternative suited him, he began investigating the cause of the rising prices.

He soon found that a number of Maine potato brokers were collaborating to drive up the price of potatoes for May delivery. Through excessive purchases, the brokers were driving the price from $8 per 100 pounds to $20 per 100 pounds. Simplot, primed for a fight, countered their maneuvers by selling 2,000 May potato futures contracts, to drive the price down to a level properly reflecting supply and demand considerations at the time. The 2,000 potato contracts represent approximatly 100 million pounds of potatoes, with a value of approximately $20 million at the time Simplot began driving the price downward.

Simplot, after selling the 2,000 contracts, had two alternatives for settling his open position with the futures exchange: (1) repurchase 2,000 contracts or (2) actually deliver 100,000,000 pounds of potatoes to the Maine brokers who bought his contracts. As the May delivery date approached, he gradually repurchased the contracts. However, he was only able to repurchase 1,000 of the 2,000. He approached the Maine brokers, offering to repurchase their contracts, but they refused to sell at the then prevailing price of $10 per 100 pounds because it would result in a significant loss for them, since they bought the contracts for between $12 and $20 per 100 pounds.

Jack then offered to deliver the equivalent of 1,000 contracts in potatoes, a total of 50 million pounds, or an astounding 1,000 rail cars of potatoes. They refused, claiming that the May contracts called for delivery of *Maine* potatoes and he was offering Idaho potatoes (a technical but legal argument). He then sent his agents to Maine to buy 50 million pounds of *Maine* potatoes to satisfy his 1,000 contracts. Trying to pressure Simplot into redeeming their contracts for at least their purchase price, the brokers had discouraged local farmers from selling to him, citing new foreign orders that would result in substantially higher prices for the farmers. Simplot found that the few potatoes he could buy could not be shipped because the Maine brokers had reserved the potato rail cars. It was a cat and mouse game that ended in May when Simplot defaulted on 1,000 potato contracts, claiming he had made every effort to settle his position but was thwarted by the brokers in their efforts to recoup their losses.

In the end, the Commodity Futures Trading Commission, the self-governing body of the futures industry, found Simplot in violation of trading practices. He paid fines and was barred from trading for five years. However, the Commission also forced the brokers to sell their remaining 1,000 contracts to Simplot for the prevailing market price of $10 per 100 pounds. It is believed that Simplot not only stabilized the price of potatoes, which he intended to do, but also netted approximately $7 million for his effort, at the expense of the brokers.

This affair has been said to have impugned Simplot's character and word, since he defaulted on 1,000 futures contracts. This author, however, represented a major bank during this period and sponsored a multi-million-dollar line of credit to the J.R. Simplot Company. The integrity, character, and resolve of Jack Simplot in the "potato war" was never questioned.

Possessiveness

As we mentioned in Chapter 1, entrepreneurs are markedly possessive about their companies, employees, and products, seeing the company as a direct extension of themselves; they don't just own the company, "they are the company." Jack Simplot's possessive nature came into play on numerous occassions as he built his Idaho-based empire, but his phosphate operation best depicts this trait.

As was pointed out earlier in this chapter, since phosphate, like many items during the war, was scarce, in traditional Simplot spirit, Jack decided to mine and process it himself. Today, the Simplot phosphate operation is one of the world's largest.

In the late 60's a friend of Simplot's, Paul Davies, president of FMC, appproached him with an offer to purchase his Pocotello phosphate processing operation, offering $2 million for this huge plant. Jack considered the offer but declined, stating, "It's a fair offer Paul, but I couldn't replace it for that and, anyhow, what do you boys want with it?" Some months later, Davies upped the FMC proposal to $12 million and Jack replied, "Gee Paul, that's a bit short, after all, it's been three months since we last discussed it." Davies' $15 million counter-offer brought another low key response, "Paul, I just can't part with it." This went on for years until Davies retired and made his last offer of $150 million, to which Jack replied, "Paul, enjoy your retirement and don't worry about my phosphate plant."

In sharing this encounter, Jack is quick to point out that

all the offers were more than fair when they were made, which prompted us to ask why he didn't sell the operation, particularly since the early offers came at a time when the company badly needed cash. He reclined in his chair, and with composed conviction, slapped his knee and bellowed, "Because they're mine and I own them lock, stock, and barrel. They are paid for and they are worth $500 million each and I own *FIVE* of them."

Recognizing the Need for Quality People

Throughout the interview with Simplot, he emphasized the critical importance of selecting and surrounding himself with quality people. "You can't do it alone, you'll beat yourself to death trying." Today the Simplot companies employ 10,000 people with an executive staff of top financial, managerial, and legal talent who coordinate operations in Germany, Thailand, Turkey, Mexico, Canada, and the United States. The operations are divided into three divisions: *Food,* which produces frozen potatoes and other vegetables and fruit products; *Minerals and Chemicals,* which mines and/or produces fertilizer, phosphate, and agri-culture chemicals; and *Land and Livestock,* which includes farms, ranches, and the nation's third largest cattle feeding operation.

Although the divisions are interrelated, they function autonomously and must pay their own way. Corporate decision making begins with the executive staff establishing objectives, with strategy left up to the division heads. "I am not involved in day-to-day activities. As chairman I have allocated those duties and my mission is to encourage people to find their own 'hunt and chase.' This makes them feel important and recognized and they feel like they own something."

Jack Simplot recognizes that he must let go, allowing others to run the day-to-day operations. But Jack still knows when and how to get involved. At the time the Micron investment was being considered by Simplot, he asked that his executives review the proposal: many were skeptical. In most U.S. corporations, the executives would have prevailed, but Simplot's vision enabled him to see the potential, just as he saw the potential for the hogs, potato sorter, and all his other ventures. The company invested and invested big in traditional Simplot fashion, "I let the boys go do it and by God they did! The structure imposed by many venture capitalists often kills the deal before it gets off the ground. You either see the potential or you don't; if you don't, stay out, and if you do, give free rein."

Independence and Control of Destiny

None of Simplot's ventures would have passed the rigors of today's self-serving corporate bureaucracy or the short-term scrutiny of today's stock market. This statement applies to Simplot's first venture in the hog business as well as to his interest in Micron Technology.

Simplot has spent his entire life in a battle for the independence to maintain control over his own destiny. For him the purpose of capital is to provide independence. Simplot is very sensitive to the importance of money, stating, "Although my purpose was not to make money, it's the way we keep score and it provides me the freedom to do what I do best, to create enterprise and pass on the entrepreneurial pursuit."

In 1928 Simplot's hog business earned him $7,800, which worked out to be $1.18 per hour over a year's period. That $7,800 built the J.R. Simplot Company, which today has sales approaching $1.5 billion and provides this Rare Breed with all the independence he could possibly ask for.

Chapter 10

*Gerald Smith
of Allied
Bankshares*

Gerald Smith of Allied Bankshares

"Creating an Environment Where the Entrepreneur Can Graze"

*G*erald Smith, the Co-founder and Chief Executive Officer of Allied Bankshares, Inc., was a reluctant interviewee because, in his words, "the bank does not operate under a star quarterback system." He compares the management approach at the bank to that of a law partnership, where the input of the partners is considered before decisions are made. Smith, however, is the "senior partner" of the team at Allied and his story about the bank, his management philosophies, and his clear thinking about the role of the bank and its objectives is an interesting one.

At Smith's insistance, management at Allied is a team effort. The Gerald Smith we write about in many ways is a composite of himself and the other team members. We ask you to keep this in mind as you read this chapter, since many times when we refer to Smith, we actually are referring to the team.

By 1972 when this story begins, Smith and his colleagues had amassed significant previous banking experience in small country banks where they learned to deal effectively with people of various races and ages in the intimacy of a rural environment.

Smith also had been influenced in his thinking by "other country boys" who provided early leadership in the state's banking growth. These included Florence from Alto, Texas

(Republic National) and Wooten from Gilmer, Texas (FBN, Dallas). Early experience as a bank examiner also convinced Smith that overregulated banks would require new efficiencies and business plans that responded to the market if they were to survive in a less regulated environment.

In 1972, Smith was looking to invest in a bank, seeking at least a 20 percent return on his investment. He states that he was, and is, a businessman first and a banker second, and as a businessman he is profit oriented. He and a few associates with similar objectives met that year "over a few drinks," and decided they would have to put their own bank together if the profit objective they had in mind was to be achieved. They founded Allied by putting two small banks together, which resulted in a combined bank with assets totaling about $250 million and profits of about $3 million. Twelve years later the assets amounted to approximately $10 billion and profits were $118 million. This track record was achieved through internal growth and by adding small banks to the group as suitable acquisitions became available. The growth was also achieved without once diluting the shareholders' equity through new stock issues. Since 1973, Allied has averaged better than a 20 percent return on stockholders' equity and is now ranked as the thirty-eighth largest bank in the country and twenty-second in profitability. Needless to say, the objectives set twelve years ago have been met. Smith is fully aware that this record will be difficult to equal over the next few years due to the changing economy in the bank's marketing area, the problems facing the petroleum industry and the supporting enterprises dependent upon that industry, and disinflation and deregulation. But, he also sees many opportunities in the free-wheeling atmosphere of the Houston area and in the rapid formation of new companies.

In 1972, Smith and his team developed a game plan for their small bank, and today, with the bank forty times larger, that same basic plan is still in effect. When the first plan was viewed by "the street," bank stock analysts thought Smith was out of his mind because the plan addressed itself primarily to the things the bank planned *not* to do, which were all the glamorous things, or, as Smith says, "the sexy things," that traditionally have intrigued bank investors and, in many instances, employees. A partial list of the activities to be left to others follows.

1) No international lending other than what was necessary to provide services for customers who were engaged in importing or exporting. Smith did not believe that a regional bank could compete effectively with the money center banks already on the scene. What Allied couldn't handle in the way of service for its customers would be referred to a money center correspondent bank. This decision made it unnecessary to open expensive overseas offices and recruit and supervise international banking executives who might very well upset the bank's other salary scales.

In retrospect, of course, Smith's decision not to enter the international banking arena was well-grounded, given the current international banking malaise. In the 1970's, many banks pursued international loans to increase loan yields and price/earning ratios to appease stockholders. In the process, they threatened the capital base of their financial institutions. Smith has chosen to stick to the fundamentals, recognizing that higher yields mean higher interest rates, which all convert to higher risk. Some of America's largest banking institutions are now realizing the truth of this fundamental principle.

2) With few exceptions, Allied avoids pursuing national accounts because the spread between the cost of money and the interest rates earned from servicing these accounts is too thin to provide the 20 percent return on equity sought by the bank. Again, this decision made it unnecessary to recruit specialized and expensive personnel and to set up a support system for assisting and supervising them. Smith observed, "There were too many ex-bankers around as treasurers, whipping the hell out of the spreads."

3) Smith considers his market area to be the eastern one-

third of Texas, where two-thirds of the state's population lives, plus Louisiana. With few exceptions, business is not sought if it doesn't fall into this geographical area.

4) Expansion through acquisitions or mergers is not undertaken just for the sake of expansion. The institution being considered as a merger or acquistion target must add to the overall performance of the group.

With the specification of these parameters, it is apparent that the bank has drawn a bead on the lower end of the "middle market" and on the special needs of the executive and professional segment of the market. This decision leaves senior executives available to personally service many clients and to make quick decisions. In banking circles, everybody discovered the "middle market" about eight or nine years ago. Smith knew it was there all the time and his bank, while vulnerable to money center bank competition, is so well entrenched that he is not greatly worried. He says, "This niche is gratifying to Allied staff entrepreneurs, who are aware this sector (the middle market) creates most of the incremental jobs in the economy, and properly served, provides built-in growth, including a loyal referral base. They are not dependant upon incremental accounts to sustain profitability."

Smith is, without a doubt, an entrepreneur, but somewhat different from many others in that he seems to have an unusual amount of self-discipline. Goals were set in 1972, along with a plan to reach those goals, and there has been no deviation from the basic plan since that time. A popular definition of an entrepreneur is someone who risks money, time, and/or reputation to reap the benefits of reaching a goal. Smith fits the definition and is enjoying the benefits. The original investors risked their capital and reputations, as well as their time, on a business plan that was counter to conventional thinking at the time and counter to most thinking today. There are many bloody noses in banking as a result of deregulation, the shrinking of basic industries, disinflation, the oil collapse, and other economic trends, so we suspect that Smith's business plan might be copied by some of the more glamorous, but less profitable, banks.

Vision and Direction

This may be Smith's strongest trait, as shown by the clear vision he and his associates had concerning the role their bank should play in the world of Texas banking, and the fact that that role still hasn't changed. After talking about the bank for about an hour and a half, describing the early thinking, the objectives, how they were reached, his philosophy regarding personnel, and many other things, Smith observed, "There is one great danger in carrying on like this, and that's the danger of believing what you say is gospel and will hold forever." The direction of the bank could change somewhat in the future, but we venture to guess that it will only be a few degrees.

Self-Confidence

The decision to launch a new bank on a limited course, in spite of advice to the contrary, is a vivid demonstration of Smith's self-confidence and decisiveness. At no time was there an attempt to test or try out some of the things that other banks were doing to make their banks all things for all people and abandoning them if they didn't work. They were simply not started in the first place. Decisiveness is reflected in the bank's policy regarding its clients. One of the bank's primary service objectives is to provide quick answers to clients' questions and requests, which is achieved by getting the bank's decision makers as close to the customers as possible.

Common Sense

This is an attribute held in high esteem by Smith and is obviously a personal trait. In developing a business plan for the bank, Smith and his associates realized that they had to start with a realistic appraisal of the abilities and experience of the people that would be available to the bank. Since Houston, at that time, was not a money center, international bankers and national account executives would have to be recruited from elsewhere. This would upset and divert management energies from a marketing strategy aimed primarily at the local low middle market segment, so they decided against what they considered to be an ego trip. In other words, their approach was, "let's keep it simple."

When screening applicants for positions at the bank, three personnel traits sought are: high energy level, high motivation, and common sense. Smith observes that this combination has turned out to be a winner over and over again.

The bank's strategies appear to be based on common sense, as evidenced by the emphasis on supplying the services the customers want instead of what the bank would like to offer. Smith realizes that they must deal with "folks", since "folks" make up a large segment of their market. He understands from talking to many customers that they want a continuing relationship with an account officer instead of having to teach a new banker about their business every six months. He also understands that customers want quick answers, so they want to deal with an officer who has clout with the loan committee. To satisfy these customer preferences, considerable decentralization is built into the system. The holding company is a service unit to the individual banks or bank clusters, "where the action is," instead of being an imperial dictator. Career paths have been deemphasized by making a move into administration financially unrewarding, so the Peter Principle doesn't have as much opportunity to operate in the Allied environment. Smith admits that the system spawns considerable lack of uniformity, further acknowledging that they don't have all the solutions to that problem and may never have. All in all, it sounds like a lot of common sense, including the recognition that it doesn't work perfectly.

Government might take a lesson from one of Allied's practices. When an important challenge arises, an ad hoc task force is formed and headed by leaders who liquidate the group when the mission is completed, thus eliminating the need for a large and expensive bureaucracy.

"We have never had to call in the management consultants to tell us what business we are in or what business we should be in. We know where our market is, and if we execute the fundamentals in a professional manner, we will succeed."

Leadership Ability

How do you convince a bank officer, who is doing a good job for the bank and for his customers, that he should stay right where he is and not try to climb the executive ladder? Hiring robots comes to mind as a possible answer, but Smith has thought of another way: Eliminate the incentive to climb the ladder by drastically compressing the salary scale between the lowest ranking, or most recently hired officer, and the chief executive.

A recent institutional research report put out by Montgomery Securities on the subject of Banking Industry Compensation confirms the unusual compensation practices at Allied. It shows that Allied pays its bankers more than other banks and that its top executives, as a group, are paid one third of the salaries of executives at the top thirty banks.

Montgomery Securities analyzed the various bank proxy statements as their source, and their analysis showed that the CEO at Allied (Smith) receives cash compensation that amounts to only 38 percent of the average CEO compensation for all Texas banks included in the study, and only 31 percent of the average for all the banks in the study. A further calculation showed that Smith's cash compensation is only 63 percent of the average compensation paid the next four officers below the Texas CEO group, and that the average for the next four officers below Smith's at Allied is only 4 percent below the CEO.

Cash compensation throughout the Allied management group is the lowest in the industry, but through several attractive stock purchase plans the Allied staff receives the highest total pay of any group of bankers in the Southwest. Net income per employee was $31,680 in 1984, compared to an industry average of $21,378 (based on one proxy statement included in the study).

This unusual compensation structure was designed to create an owner/operator culture and align the employees interests with those of shareholders. With 87 percent of eligible employees owning stock in the company, Allied has even been able to collapse the company pension plan. Employees are building net worth each year and everybody has a stake in the success of the company. Instead of being the poorest paid CEO in banking, Gerald Smith's 1,000,000-plus shares make him one of the best paid, with dividend income of over $900,000 a year. We quote from the closing sentence of the Montgomery Securities report in reference to Allied's compensation plan, "We only wish there were greater evidence of owner-management at the helm of the companies we follow."

High Energy and Drive

People who have achieved success are often the objects of envy and are considered by many to have been lucky in the investments they have made. While luck, insofar as timing is concerned, may have played a part, nearly all the entrepreneurs we interviewed attributed their success to a high level of energy and motivation inspired by a belief in what they were doing. Robert Mondavi, chairman of the Mondavi Winery, observed that too many people give up before reaching their goals because of lack of energy. Gerald Smith has the necessary energy and motivation, and these two qualities, along with common sense, are the two other traits sought in all new employees joining Allied. I.Q. scores are important, of course, but they don't make up for the other qualities.

The banking industry has experienced wrenching changes since 1970 due to gradual deregulation, an awakening to the pure commodity nature of money, massive loan losses and bank closures, and, in select cases, major embarrassments to the industry as a result of fraud, mismanagement, and improperly structured and documented loans. It has been our observation as corporate/international financial consultants and former bankers that the industry, in general, is reactionary, with a short-term mentality based on quarterly reports and stockholder pressure. Further, it is an industry that generally does not encourage entrepreneurship because of its rigid "policies" and massive bureaucracies.

Allied, under the stewardship of Smith and his associates, has minimized bureaucracy and encouraged an entrepreneurial spirit by combining salaries with stock incentives. As a result, the bank encourages collective problem solving and commitment from its people, a refreshing difference from other banks. It has enabled Smith and Allied to maintain its superior performance despite the rapidly declining price of oil in its Houston-Louisana market area, a remarkable entrepreneurial achievement for this Rare Breed.

Chapter 11

*Don Tyson
of Tyson Foods
Inc.*

Don Tyson
of Tyson Foods
Inc.

"Vision to Manage Change and Allocate the Entrepreneurial Spirit"

*A*s chairman of Tyson Foods Inc., Don Tyson is responsible for taking this hay and chicken hauling company, founded in 1935 by his father, from $1 million in sales in 1952 to $1.1 billion in 1985. Under his leadership, Tyson Foods has become the largest integrated poultry processing company in the United States. It had a 20 percent after tax return on equity in 1984-85, ranking it number one in the Fortune 500 and number eight over a ten-year period. In addition, Tyson has been profitable in twenty-four of the last twenty-five years and has come through the most vicious industry downturn as a larger and stronger company, while many competitors filed bankruptcy.

Exploring the characteristics that motivated Tyson's incredible achievements allows us to examine how he and his cadre managed change, as opposed to merely reacting to it, in a knee-jerk fashion. The Tyson story also reveals the importance of planning systems as integrated, ongoing, and dynamic components of an entrepreneurial corporate culture.

The Industry

To more fully appreciate Tyson's achievements we will briefly explore the U.S. poultry industry.

Tyson's fully integrated poultry processing operation purchases grain ingredients, mills the feed, and delivers it along with baby chicks to independent/contract growers. After eight weeks, the mature birds are returned to Tyson for processing and market delivery. Tyson is unique in that it takes the concept of integrated processing to its logical conclusion with a highly successful marketing and sales program featuring ready-to-cook entrees for retail sales. The company also is a major supplier of chicken chunks and patties to the fast food industry.

Like the beef and pork industries, the poultry industry is involved in the efficient conversion of feed to meat. However, there are marked differences among the various meat industries. While it takes one and a half to two years for a steer to mature for market, it takes eight weeks for a chicken to mature; while it takes eight pounds of feed to create one pound of beef, it only takes two pounds of feed to yield one pound of chicken meat; while it takes eight to twenty acres to graze one steer, 25,000 chickens are raised in a 60' × 150' space. And finally, there is a highly regulated commodity futures market that can protect beef producers' price fluctuations, whereas the poultry industry has no such hedging mechanism.

Until recently, the poultry industry was production oriented, processing whole birds and cut-up parts for consumers. The absence of a finished product hedging mechanism forced the poultry producer to sell his product at the prevailing market price, thus exposing himself to losses. Further reducing direct control over pricing is a ten-day product perishability period. There are hedging mechanisms to minimize feed cost fluctuations which represent about 50 percent of the average break-even cost of processing chicken. However, when a producer hedges feed but cannot hedge the final product, it gains no real advantage.

Consumer trends have dramatically changed poultry processing from a production oriented industry to a marketing/ retail focused one. This has resulted in a greater emphasis on product mix to meet changes in consumer demand. Don Tyson, early on, understood the importance of this nascent trend and became a leader in producing consumer/market driven poultry products. Today the industry provides three basic products:

1) *Commodity:* Whole bird or cut-up parts where there are thin margins and where price is uncontrollable, given the pure commodity nature.

2) *Value-added:* Deboned product where price is comparatively stable and where the product is often produced under a cost-plus arrangement for another merchandiser of the product. An example is chicken nuggets sold to fast food operations.

3) *Further-processed:* Packaged product ready for the retail consumer, where retail price is relatively stable but where margins fluctuate based on the variable cost of feed.

The following table shows the ten-year production trend for these three basic product areas.

October Weekly Production
Millions of Pounds

	Commodity	Value-Added	Further Processed	Total
1974	458	227	55	740
	62%	31%	7%	100%
1984	455	545	204	1,204
	38%	45%	17%	100%

For the ten-year period, total weekly production increased 464 million pounds, from 740 million to 1,204 million, which represents a growth of 63 percent and attests to the increase in poultry consumption. Whole bird and ice packed products, which represent the commodity category, remained stable in terms of pounds produced, but declined significantly relative to total production. In 1974, the commodity category represented 62 percent of output, but decreased substantially in 1984, accounting for only 38 percent of production, a 39 percent decline in contribution to total production.

As commodity products in absolute terms declined slightly over the period, value-added deboned meat, in contrast, more than doubled from 227 million to 545 million weekly pounds. This 140 percent absolute increase percent represented a 45 percent increase relative to its contribution to total output, which increased from 31 percent of the total to 45 percent. The greatest percentage increase, however, came from the further-processed products category. In 1974, 55 million weekly pounds were produced, representing 7 percent of total output, but by 1984, 204 million pounds were produced (an absolute increase of 271 percent), contributing 17 percent to total output. As the numbers indicate, the emphasis has clearly been on the value-added, further-processed products. This trend has resulted from the following:

- Fast food chains expanded volume and featured poultry products such as chicken nuggets and patties.

- The low fat content of chicken has led consumers to begin eating more poultry. A greater variety of poultry menu applications also has helped to increase consumption. The 1985 *Better Homes and Gardens Cook Book* has twenty pages of poultry dishes while there are twelve pages each for beef and pork dishes.

- The increase in the number of working women and the wide use of microwave cooking has led consumer preferences to shift toward readily consumable products.

- Poultry remains the lowest priced meat.

For these reasons, per capita poultry consumption has substantially increased. It equaled pork in 1985 and is expected to equal beef consumption in 1990.

Meat Consumption
Pounds Per Person

Year	Poultry	Pork	Beef	Total
1978	45	62	123	230
	20%	27%	53%	100%
1985	60	60	97	217
	28%	28%	45%	100%

In the 1978-85 period, overall per capita meat consumption declined 6 percent, primarily at the expense of beef. Pork remained relatively stable but beef's share of the consumers' meat diet declined 16 percent, whereas poultry increased 33 percent. Although Tyson does not claim responsibility for these trends, he has certainly capitalized on it. He is considered the pace setter, though he acknowledges that it was consumer preferences that increased poultry demand.

The fast food industry, has also provided an opportunity for Don Tyson. He is the largest provider of chicken chunks and patties to the fast food market, letting the fast food industry develop the market for him and take all the financial risks.

What has contributed to the company's success in all market segments, as well as to its overall financial performance? Don Tyson's statement, "If we don't produce the very best then I don't have anything to talk about," begins to shed some light on the answer to this question.

Recognize and Promote Quality People

Tyson graduated from college and joined his father's company in 1952, at which time the firm was processing 10,000 chickens a week, with annual sales of one million dollars. Today, sales exceed a billion dollars and Tyson processes 11 million chickens weekly. When he joined Tyson Foods there were fifty-two employees, today there are 22,000 employees and 6,000 poultry growers, making the Tyson family 28,000 people strong.

Don Tyson does not view the human element of business in the abstract, as many theorists have, including Adam Smith. He emphasizes that his responsibility is to provide a working environment that is enjoyable, and that encourages people to excel through pride of association with his company. He encourages open communications at every level and openly appreciates the fact that all his people are key in helping him capture the critical environmental information he needs to make timely and correct decisions.

At Tyson, the entrepreneurial spirit is available for all to participate in who want to. Tyson and his executives identify corporate objectives and strategies, by which achievement is measured; but the actual process and the details of executing the plan, are left up to the individuals. Tyson emphasizes this when he says "There are a thousand ways to skin a cat and I don't care how it's done as long as it's accomplished." His people have, therefore, a true sense of contributing to the company's performance, with 18 percent of the Tyson stock owned by the employees. With this freedom to execute corporate plans comes the responsiblity to achieve. As Tyson reminds his employees, "If you ever wonder whose responsibility it is to do the job, it's yours!"

Tyson is tolerant of mistakes, encourages open and candid communications, and quickly redirects efforts when such is called for. His open communications policy discourages cover-up of errors and encourages proper attention without reprisal. "People make mistakes, that's life, but we learn from these errors and bring them to the surface; we don't bury them. To truly be entrepreneurial, you have to learn to let go and provide your people with the opportunity to make their own mistakes."

Although Tyson encourages intercompany competition, he does not tolerate the kind of intercompany rivalries that can become destructive. "We provide contests and rewards but we discourage self-enhancement at the expense of another division. We have plenty of outside competition to fight and I admire the person who sacrifices his/her own position for the good of the overall effort." The fact that Tyson is one of the best performing companies in America attests to the validity of this approach and attitude. The open communications and team spirit are an inherent part of the Tyson culture. Don attributes this approach to his father. "He encouraged me to challenge new areas and accept the risks and rewards of my actions."

Don expresses a profound pride in and responsibility for his people. "They must enjoy their work and find satisfaction in their contribution. To do this, they need to feel they own something and are recognized for their contribution. That's why we let them skin the cat their way, it encourages success, ownership, and creative solutions in a positive way."

Don Tyson has created and nurtured a working environment that recognizes the importance of people and their abilities to be creative and to some extent, visionary. This is fortified through various incentive programs and employee stock ownership opportunities, as noted above.

Planning

People in agribusiness are accustomed to change. Capricious environmental factors that have no effect on other industries are simply a way of life for the agribusiness. The industry's culture is geared toward change and, more importantly, to the management and direction of change. These people are, of necessity, resourceful, as they must continually strive to maintain some semblance of economic equilibrium.

Tyson's ability to respond to and capitalize on market changes is demonstrative of his ability to manage and redirect corporate resources. The structural changes required to meet the recent wave of record consumer demand were undertaken in the midst of one of the most severe downturns in the industry's history, during which many poultry firms went into bankruptcy. Tyson not only weathered these storms but emerged stronger. He doubled production with the acquisition of VALMAC Industries, a firm purchased from the Bass brothers, who acquired it from Lane Processing under Chapter 11 of the Bankruptcy Code. What is remarkable is that in the face of one of the industry's worst slumps, and during a period of changing consumer demands, Tyson acquired a major poultry operation, thus doubling its size, while posting the best return on equity among the Fortune 500 companies in 1985. An amazing achievement!

Be assured, this just did not happen, but resulted from constant and careful planning. Planning is a discipline, requiring continued and collective attention. For the most part, we find that companies plan only in the face of adversity, which is often too late, or they plan once a year, as a matter of ritual. However, the problem with these methods is that they fail to recognize that the only certainty is uncertainty, and that contingencies often arise randomly at any time of the year. The "traditional" yearly planning effort assumes the operating environment to be static, when in fact it is dynamic and constantly changing. A company that is not constantly planning will either lose or fall short of its potential; most certainly it could not endure the hardships faced by Tyson and emerge victorious. To quote Harold Geneen in his book *Managing,* "Management's purpose is to manage," and this is where planning begins.

Like other disciplines, such as golf or tennis, planning needs to be a practiced corporate process. The professional golfer hits balls every day, not just before a tournament, and the professional manager needs to be involved with data gathering and planning efforts in the same way.

The following flow chart identifies the strategic planning process. The numbers correspond with the narrative, following the chart.

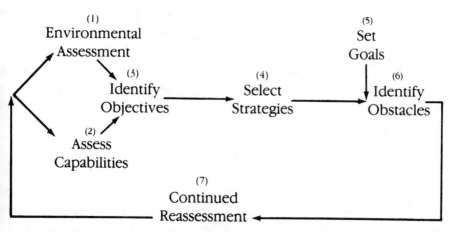

1) *Environmental Assessment:* This is a collective management function during which the present operating environment is explored and future changes and their probable impact are identified. Naturally, the longer the time horizon, the more elusive the contingencies. Anticipation and monitoring are required for managing the outcome. Environmental analysis should cover market trends such as those discussed earlier (consumer's demand for more value-added and readily consumable products). It should cover competition, government regulation, and assess complementary products like beef and pork. It should also include a thorough review of the economy, interest rates, and the value of the dollar relative to other currencies, which could affect imports or exports. This is a process of assessment, corporate radar whose purpose it is to capture vital information.

A word about competition is in order. There is a natural tendency to focus on outside competition. Although this needs to be noted and observed, it can also create illusions within a company's management and compromise goal setting. When a company bases its progress on the performance of competitors, it may be limiting its potential or may attempt to attain the unachievable, given its capabilities. Also, today's competition may not be tomorrow's. An example is the banking industry, where numerous "nonbanking" organizations are actively competing for consumer and industrial credit. Major competitors for the banking industry must include Sears, the giant retailer; McDonell Douglas, the aircraft manufacturer; G.E., the appliance producer; as well as the credit arms of the big three automobile manufacturers.

2) *Capabilities:* This is an internal assessment, requiring nonbiased review of tangible and intangible resources. It should focus on the strengths and weaknesses of management itself, manpower, market position, and other such areas. This is a critical second step to identifying objectives. Companies where open communication is encouraged, such as at Tyson, are best equipped for this honest and nonjudgmental process. Where candid communication is not encouraged, accuracy will be negatively affected. Either the capabilities are overstated and objectivies become unattainable, or the capabilities are understated and the corporate potential is not achieved, resulting in frustration, low morale and high employee turnover. In either event, the entire planning process is misdirected.

3) *Objectives:* Corporate objectives are based on a realistic assessment of the environment and the firm's capabilities. Successful planning discourages quantifying objectives. Instead of focusing just on numbers, objectives should reflect the future of the organization and form a common and well-defined rallying point for performance. For Tyson, this is reflected in the slogan, "Doing our best just for you"; for Ford Motor Company, it is "Quality is Job One"; for Weatherby it is "Tomorrow's Firearms Today." These statements are not ambiguous, cannot be manipulated to suit circumstances, and are a constant reminder of the firm's collective effort for the employee and for the customer.

Companies that quantify their objectives inevitably encourage their managers to become too obsessed with the numbers to the point that the forest cannot be distinguished clearly from the trees. As Tyson says, "We watch the numbers very carefully, but more importantly, *we look through* the numbers at what affects them. The numbers by themselves are meaningless unless you understand the background." If the sole corporate objective is to achieve 20 percent return on equity, the firm will lose the commitment of its employees, many of whom will not understand what it means. However, given an objective of "Doing our best just for you (the customer)," the person responsible for cleaning the Tyson truck fleet knows precisely what is expected and will take pride in how every Tyson poultry tractor and trailer looks. Although the truck washer may not be directly involved in contributing to return on equity, he is directly involved in maintaining the image of the "best just for you." It conveys an attitude and a universal rallying point for each employee to understand the contribution he or she can make. Tyson's experience shows that when you have "The Best," sell "The Best," and deliver "The Best," you are the odds-on favorite to be the best and, by doing that, a 20 percent return on equity can be attained. It's no accident!

The assessment of the environment, the analysis of corporate capabilities, and the establishment of objectives fall into the domain of management. However, the identification of strategies, the establishment of goals against which success is measured, the monitoring of obstacles, and continued reassessment require a joint effort involving management and employees. By including employee input, management also encourages employee commitment to the final outcome. The fleet manager at Tyson has a better idea of truck washing requirements than Don Tyson, after all, that's why Tyson hired him. Therefore, when goals are set, Tyson consults with his department heads, who in turn consult with their people. The result is attainable standards of measurement and a commitment to attain them by the employees who set them.

4) *Strategies:* Once objectivies are identified and communicated to every level, the middle managers identify specific strategies for achieving the objectives. These are laid out much as an army would strategize taking a hill or gun emplacement. These strategies differ from division to division but will eventually provide a common understanding of achievement. It is a well-orchestrated and clearly communicated plan of attack that takes into account the corporate environment, its capabilities, and objectives. If the assessment of these areas is inaccurate, then the strategy will be misdirected.

5) *Goals:* These are established to measure the success of the strategies in meeting objectives. For the most part they are quantitative. This is a critical area in the overall process *since the goals become employee objectives.* Unlike traditional corporate objective setting, which is often thematic and lacking in detail, goals are precise and thoroughly understood by the parties whose responsibility it will be to see that the stated goals are met. Further, as managers and employees contribute to the goal setting process, there is a "grass roots" commitment to seeing that goals are reached.

A word on goal achievement is in order. People who *constantly* exceed their goals are not setting them high enough in the first place. People who *constantly* underachieve are not properly assessing their environment and/or capabilities. Finally, people who *constantly* hit their goals may be playing with the numbers. That is why Don Tyson and his team look beyond the numbers. They encourage open and candid communications to obtain accurate and meaningful data upon which to base well-grounded decisions.

6) *Obstacles:* Any well run business actively recognizes that there will not always be smooth sailing. Contingencies and obstacles are an inherent part of business. The key to preventing such obstacles from rendering the strategies and

even the objectives obsolete is to pre-identify alternative approaches or contingencies. Tyson's grain buyer, for example, can't peg the exact feed cost in six months anymore than the president of a bank can tell you what interest rates will be. What they can do is constantly monitor and report trends and identify alternatives and solicit expert opinions. They begin by asking "what if" questions, exploring various scenarios and assigning various probabilities to likely contingencies. An accurate management information system is most important and one of management's responsibilities is to establish an internal communications network that facilitates and captures critical data in a timely manner.

7) *Reassessment:* This is a team effort. This process makes the Tyson planning system dynamic and ongoing, recognizing the fact that effective planning, like the environment, is not static. It's alive and constantly changing, posing obstacles and presenting opportunities. Tyson exploits opportunities and manages obstacles because its planning system has built-in flexibility, and the people have pride of ownership, knowing that achievement will be fully recognized. This environment didn't just "hatch" for Tyson Foods; it is the corporate culture established by Don Tyson and by his father — a winning legacy whose performance is admired by many corporations and competitors. The results, of course, are self-evident!

At Tyson, open communication is so strongly encouraged that it is even applied to the dress code. Most people, including Don Tyson, wear Khaki pants and shirts with the Tyson logo. This reflects a family spirit and a company-wide commitment to the companies goals.

Perpetual Achievement

Tyson states, "In my life, there has always been a mountain to climb and conquer. When you finish one mountain you are eager to see the next and the next. It's a never ending quest to achieve, it's excitingly perpetual and a driving force."

Achievement and recognition represent the purpose, while vision is the process—vision to see beyond today and through environmental constraints and structures. "We spend today's dollars for tomorrow's progress." This statement is part and parcel of the Tyson culture and helps explain why his company seriously intends to dominate and control over 50 percent of its markets.

Sales and Promotional Skills

Don Tyson not only promotes his many products, but has developed a highly sophisticated marketing approach. By purchasing advertising independent of the retail stores that carry his products, Tyson's products receive considerable attention and consumer notice. This form of independent marketing encourages the consumer to request retailers to carry Tyson products.

It is important to note that for the most part, retail prices for Tyson poultry have remained relatively stable. Unlike most companies, which depend on inflated prices, Tyson's remarkable profit performance has been based on improving efficiency and expanding product applications; it has not relied on price inflation for growth.

Quality is the hallmark of Tyson's sales and promotion strategy; "If we don't produce and deliver the very best product, then I don't have anything to talk about."

Competition

"Without competition there would be no game and no purpose. Can you imagine a football team suiting up for a noncompetitive game." Competition is not only welcome, it is strongly encouraged. For Don Tyson it means progress and it keeps "my team in shape." His competitive spirit is seen in his hobby, sport fishing. Here, Tyson tests his skills and strategies against trophy fish. Yet once he has won the battle, he releases the catch for another day. His is a true spirit of healthy competition, which he tries to instill in his people. For him, the sport and the chase are the achievements, and his style underscores the importance of restraint and patience. This spirit was clearly shown in his acquisition of VALMAC Industries, which made Tyson number one in total poultry sales.

Just how competitive Don Tyson is, and just how determined he can be, is well illustrated by the VALMAC acquistion. From 1980 to 1984, the poultry industry experienced its most protracted downturn in history. At the time, Lane Processing was the largest poultry processor in the United States and Tyson was ranked fifth. Clift and Dorothy Lane, the founders of Lane Processing, had agreed to sell their company to Tyson, but at the last moment backed out of the deal.

In 1982, the Lanes borrowed $9 million from Worthen Bank to subsidize Lane's cash flow. This loan was collateralized by the stock the Lanes held in VALMAC Industries. In November 1982, the $9 million loan matured. According to the Lanes, "The bank agreed to roll-over the loan if the interest was brought current. After paying the interest, the bank legally sold the $9 million note and underlying collateral to Stephens Inc., a major investment banking house. Stephens, in turn, sold the note and underlying collateral to Tyson."

On November 1, 1982, Tyson demanded payment on the $9 million note and threatened to take over VALMAC, which was valued at approximately $35 million, if the payment was not made. On November 2, 1982, Lane filed under Chapter 11 of the Federal Bankruptcy Code in order to protect its assets. At the time this was the largest agribusiness bankruptcy in U.S. history.

In April 1983 the bankruptcy court in Greensboro, North Carolina, under Judge James Wolfe, ordered the sale of VALMAC. The company was sold to the Bass Brothers of Fort Worth, Texas, for approximately $35 million. The following year, Tyson paid $55 million for VALMAC.

In August 1984 Lane emerged with a confirmed Plan of Reorganization. One year later, unable to comply with the court ordered plan, Clift and Dorothy Lane relinquished their positions and their stock in Lane. In the spring of 1986, Tyson bought the rest of Lane's operations for $35 million, making Tyson number one. "When it comes to competition in the poultry industry, I am the most effective son-of-a-bitch in the game."

Tyson's personal view of competition is also illustrated by a story he frequently tells. "Two campers were discussing what to do in the event a bear charged their camp. One camper said he would run like hell. His buddy noted, 'How are you going to outrun the bear, he's faster than you?' The first camper replied, 'I don't have to outrun the bear, I just have to outrun you.'"

With Don Tyson, we have a rare opportunity to explore the entrepreneur under extreme circumstances; when he directed his company through the worst recession in the industry's history; when he made major capital outlays to meet changes in consumer demand; and when the company doubled production, making it the largest poultry-based processor. Meeting any one of these challenges would be a major achievement for any businessman, much less experiencing *all three at the same time*. What is remarkable is that the company, under Tyson's stewardship, met these challenges and maintained its financial integrity.

Adam Smith, when attempting to define the essence of entrepreneurship in *The Wealth of Nations,* stressed risk taking and the marshalling of land, labor, and capital. Today's entrepreneur, as exemplified by Don Tyson, posesses certain traits that far exceed this traditional definition. We have seen little evidence of "risk taking", in the sense of speculation, in any of our interviews including the one with Tyson. For the most part, today's entrepreneurs make every effort to thoroughly identify and manage potential risks. And, when possible, to shift the capital risks to third party investors.

Vision to see beyond structure; *creativity* to manage and direct change; *patience* to capitalize on proper timing; *ability to recognize and motivate people; resourcefulness* in managing assets while employing efficient planning systems; *promotional skills,* with the emphasis on pride of ownership and product quality; *competitiveness,* with the sport and the chase as driving forces; and *achievement,* these are the elements of Tyson's highly regarded success. Don Tyson personifies the new breed of entrepreneur, employing sophisticated management techniques to exploit opportunity in face of change.

Chapter 12

*Roy Weatherby
of Weatherby
(Firearms) Inc.*

Roy Weatherby
of Weatherby
(Firearms) Inc.

*"You Must Persevere
and Sacrifice"*

"*I* was pleased to learn that you are celebrating 40 years in business. You can take great pride in your work. Stories like yours are encouraging and inspiring, for it is hard working individuals like you that make the backbone of this nation."

> Signed—
> Ronald Reagan 5/17/85
> President
> (Weatherby Rifle Owner)

As the founder and chairman of Weatherby Inc., manufacturer of premier firearms and ammunition, Roy Weatherby celebrated forty years of business and his seventy-fifth birthday in 1985. The unofficial ambassador of the firearms industry, Weatherby's achievements are legendary. The name "Weatherby" speaks of a forty-year tradition of excellence in firearms manufacturing and of the uncompromising quality, integrity, and credibility of the man. The advancements he has made in the firearms industry, especially in the precision and the stunning appearance of the firearms his company manufacturers, are part and parcel of the Weatherby legend. Although often copied, Weatherby firearms' appearance and performance are uniquely Weatherby. "We build and sell premier rifles and shotguns, which are safe, reliable, and precision hunting firearms, providing sportsmen with pride and distinction." Firearms are bought to be displayed as much as to be used, and a "Weatherby" in a sportsman's gun cabinet is a statement in and of itself.

Vision

For Weatherby, the concept of vision has been incorporated into his company's mission statement, "Tomorrow's Firearms Today!"

"Seeing your dream come true is the highest ambition that I can truthfully say I've realized. For forty years we have brought hunters the best. Each product has been designed to provide flawless performance and rugged reliability. You can count on it hunt after hunt and year after year; that's the Weatherby commitment."

When Weatherby began he was not satisfied with the ammunition and firearms available on the market at the time, believing that major ballistic and design improvements could be accomplished. "I always loved to study ballistics, and I was curious as a boy; I didn't understand why the second bullet didn't go into the same target hole made by the first bullet." This curosity about inconsistent performance eventually resulted in the development of the most efficient and prestigious firearms and ammunition in the industry.

Like so many other entrepreneurs, Weatherby initially set out simply to satisfy his own curiosity, but had the foresight to see the eventual application for others. "Most people simply don't have ideas. I had design ideas that were correct, and I had the conviction that they were right. I also had tenacity and the ability to stick to it, particularly during financially troubled periods, which were many. I wasn't the only person experimenting with ballistics in 1937, but I guess my drive to achieve kept me going."

Although he attended the University of Wichita at night, he didn't complete his education due to the onset of the

Depression. His love of ballistics endured, however, and in 1937, at the age of twenty-seven, he began to explore various theories he had concerning ammunition. "I was experimenting with various cartridge shapes and sizes along with different powders and bullets. In 1944, I had the opportunity to field test my ideas on a deer hunting trip in Utah."

Prior to his Utah trip in 1944, Weatherby had read an article by Major Charles Askins Sr., firearms editor for *Field and Stream* magazine. At that time, Askins accused the wildcatters (handloaders experimenting with ballistics) of "doodling with no apparent worthwhile effort in mind." The article suggested that optimal ballistic performance had been achieved by the major manufacturers. Roy knew better. Although he did not originate the idea of higher velocity ammunition with greater destructive power, he was able to perfect it through his extensive experiments. And he promoted it. At that time, the emphasis was on bullet size and weight for killing power, whereas Weatherby's efforts focused on bullet speed. "Many others were experimenting with velocity but apparently didn't have the perseverance to follow it through."

The 1944 deer hunting trip was Weatherby's first field test of his theories. He found that his cartridge, a .270 magnum, shot faster and flatter than commercial ammunition. This resulted in a flatter trajectory and increased killing power. As a hunter and conservationist, Weatherby was most concerned about a quick and humane kill. This critical deer hunting trip proved his theories of speed, accuracy, and quick kill, which he submitted to *Field and Stream* in response to Major Charles Askins' earlier article. To his surprise, the rebuttal was published and the reader response was overwhelming. This resulted in Weatherby's departure from his then successful insurance career and the eventual development of the highly regarded Weatherby line of firearms and ammunition.

The *Field and Stream* article and Weatherby's response illustrates another major trait we found in many entrepreneurs— being opportunistic as to luck and timing. Weatherby had no influence over the release of Askins' article in *Field and Stream*, and he certainly didn't have control over the magazine's printing of his rebuttal. But he did have the vision and conviction to seize the opportunity and pursue his ideas based on the level of reader response to his article. "Any honest person would have to admit that luck plays a big role, but the entrepreneur has to know what the proper timing is, and move quickly."

Forty years after this incident, Weatherby wrote, "It is apparent that the controversy between heavy bullets and high velocity has really ended. Over the past few decades, the public has accepted, without question, the fact that velocity plays a far greater role in humane and instant kills. Slowly, and perhaps too slowly, we have advanced. . . . And now, many years after the first Weatherby high velocity cartridges appeared on the market, other arms companies have followed. There seems to be little question today that the hunter has accepted the fact that high velocity is far more deadly at any reachable range than the big bore, slow moving, heavy projectiles of yesterday. Due to the dynamic shocking power of high velocity, it is not absolutely essential that the animal be hit in a vital spot in order to make a one-shot kill. Far too many times, with inadequate firearms, an animal is merely wounded. This results in the hunter conscientiously spending hours tracking the game, and the animal suffers a lingering death."

Possessiveness and Achievement

As we noted in Chapter 1, the entrepreneur sees his company and its products as an extension of himself, and as such he is possessive of both. Often the very characteristics of the product are a reflection and expression of the individual's own values. Weatherby firearms range in price from $550 to $4,000, representing the high end of the market. "I could build a cheaper product but it just wouldn't be a Weatherby, now would it? From the beginning I was dedicated to building the best."

After designing new cartridges that out-performed commercial ammunition, Weatherby began designing a new rifle, which was eventually introduced as the Mark V. Like his ammunition, he built his rifle because of his dissatisfaction with existing firearms. "There really hadn't been much progress made in the firearms industry and it just kept producing the same products." After World War II, no commercial rifle actions were available, so Weatherby scavenged and used whatever could be found. The early Weatherbys were distinctive in appearance, and were chambered for high-speed Weatherby ammunition, but the actions were varied: Mauser, Springfield, Enfield, Remington, Winchester, and others were used. Sometimes, in fact, he would cannibalize a customer's existing rifle for the action he needed to build a custom Weatherby.

In order to expand volume, Weatherby needed a steady and reliable source of actions. New tooling and gauges were prohibitively expensive in America. In 1948, he met with representatives of F.N. Mauser with whom he reached an agreement for them to produce a bolt action for Weatherby rifles. He now had a steady stock of Mauser actions, and was producing his own barrels. In 1950 he re-designed the rifles exquisite walnut stock, which has become a hallmark of the Weatherby rifle.

Still, however, Weatherby owners were handloading ammunition, since none was commercially available. In 1953, Weatherby traveled to Norma Ammunition Company in Sweden and persuaded it to produce the famous Weatherby cartridges. It was at this point that he became a viable force in the arms industry, offering both rifles and commercial ammunition.

In 1958 he began manufacuring his self-designed, now famous Weatherby Mark V action, which incorporated many new design ideas and safety features never incorporated in a rifle before. For instance, his bolt action, considered the strongest on the market, with nine locking lugs compared to two for most rifles; a completely shrouded bolt sleeve to eliminate gas leaks and consequential eye damage; and a 40 percent shorter throw for efficient and quicker bolt opening. Because of these and many other design contributions, Weatherby is considered by many to have produced more "firsts" in the arms industry than any other arms company in the past hundred years.

In addition, his contributions have been the most copied.

Because of capital limitations and the enormous cost of retooling, Weatherby moved the production of his action first to Germany and then in the 1970's to Japan, where all his rifles and shotguns are now manufactured.

Promotion and Desire for Recognition

Weatherby is the most recognized promoter of the firearms industry in general and his company in particular.

Like Helen Boehm, the producer of the finest art porcelain, Weatherby has always tried to associate his products with highly visible personalities: celebrities, statesmen and royalty. Notables have included President Reagan, John Wayne, and Gary Cooper. When the President of the United States gives a rifle to a Head of State, it is usually a Weatherby. Russia's Nikita Kruschev, for example, was to receive a Weatherby commissioned by President Dwight D. Eisenhower. However, Kruschev's shoe-pounding antics and his threat "we will bury you" not only heightened the cold war but resulted in no Weatherby rifle for Kruschev!

Weatherby early on recognized that Winchester and Remington were dominant forces in the industry. So he built firearms for the high end of the market. In the 1980's, to further strengthen its market position, Ed Weatherby, Roy's son and the current president of the company, introduced the new Weatherby Fibermark, thereby expanding the rifle line. Also, without compromising quality or styling, three new Vanguard models were introduced to compete with competitive guns in the lower price range.

The Fibermark was another Weatherby "first." It's hand embedded fiberglass stock retains the distinctive Weatherby styling, and the rifle incorporates the famed Mark V action. This product is unique in that the fiberglass stock makes it impervious to changes in climate, resulting in greater stability and accuracy.

Another promotional thrust of Roy Weatherby's over the

years has resulted from his avid interest and prowess in hunting. He holds many world records with trophies won on every continent, which has helped establish credibility for his products among serious hunters around the globe.

When considering the traits that led to his considerable personal and professional achievements, Weatherby firmly states that a driving force was his need "to be recognized" for his contributions. "It was important to me to achieve where others had failed. Others were experimenting with ballistics, and the basic concepts of velocity were known, but I guess I had more determination to excel and persevere." This tenacity to achieve and be recognized is a necessary ingredient for all successful entrepreneurs, and is what helps them turn their visions into reality. Weatherby describes it as "vanity or ego gratification, with recognition the reward for the sacrifices and the loneliness in achieving what others don't."

Weatherby's appreciation for the importance of recognition in most people's motivations resulted in his creation thirty years ago of the famed Weatherby Big Game Trophy. This annual award is considered the "Oscar" of the hunting industry. A distinguished panel presents the award to the person who has made outstanding contributions to the sport of big game hunting, to conservation, and to hunter education and whose character and sportsmanship are beyond reproach. It is one of the most coveted trophies in sports.

For Roy Weatherby, the recognition of his contributions have been many. In 1976, the Hunting Hall of Fame Foundation conferred upon him its "Highest Distinction" award. "This select honor is bestowed upon the individual whose interests, works, acts and achievements, in performance and by example, significantly contribute to our American hunting practices and traditions."

At his seventy-fifth birthday and fortieth year in business celebration party, attended by some of the hunting world's most prestigious dignitaries, the National Rifle Association, representing over three million members, presented the following resolution to Roy Weatherby:

"WHEREAS, Roy Edward Weatherby, Sr., Founder, Owner and Chairman of the Board of Weatherby, Inc. is celebrating his 75th birthday and his company's 40th anniversary; and

WHEREAS, He has devoted his life, skills, and expertise to a career of service to the free world's hunters, resulting in some of the finest modern big game hunting rifles, shotguns, cartridges, ammunition, and other hunting related products; and

WHEREAS, He designed and manufactured glamorous hunting rifles, purchased by numerous famous personalities including John Wayne, Gary Cooper, and Burt Lancaster; and

WHEREAS, In 1956, he created the famed Weatherby Big Game Trophy to provide recognition to hunters who make valuable contributions to the chase, to conservation, hunter education, and good sportsmanship; and

WHEREAS, He is one of the world's most accomplished and recognized hunters and leading conservationists, has hunted on four continents, has taken hundreds of trophies and remains in the Records of North America Big Game for bagging a record book polar bear trophy in 1959; and

WHEREAS, Weatherby, Inc. was designated by Los Angeles Olympic Organizing Committee as the exclusive licensee to produce 1,000 limited-edition rifles commemorating the 1984 Olympic Games; now, therefore, be it

RESOLVED, That the Board of Directors of the National Rifle Association of America, in meeting assembled this twenty-second day of April, 1985, hereby expresses its gratitude, appreciation, and congratulations to Roy Weatherby, Sr. for his outstanding contributions in the hunting and conservation fields on the occasion of his 75th birthday and his company's 40th anniversay; and, be it further

RESOLVED, That this resolution be spread upon the minutes of the meeting and that a copy, suitably embossed, be presented to Roy Edward Weatherby, Sr.''

This acknowledgement from one of the largest industry groups in the U.S. not only underscores Weatherby's individual contributions to the firearms industry, but it also acknowledges his life-long promotion of the sport of hunting and of conservationism. It's a broad and sweeping testimonial to the works of a balanced entrepreneur who has effectively and relentlessly promoted his company, its products, and the industry and whose obsession to achieve has left its mark on all three.

Self-Confidence and Perseverance to Overcome Obstacles

The Weatherby story, as we touched on before, brings into view many well known people, such as General Twining; General Lemay; General Robert Scott, who wrote *God Is My Co-Pilot;* John Wayne; Gary Cooper; Robert Taylor; Robert Stack; Ronald Reagan; and numerous sports figures and social and political leaders. However, it is also a story filled with hardship and sacrifice, as Weatherby recounts: "These past forty years have taken their toll because there were too many of those years where the worry, anxiety, and problems were almost unbelievable. The long hours and many days that I had to put in for so many years.... Consequently, today I feel older than I look, for it has been a hard life.''

Born in Kansas in 1910, the son of a poor tenant farmer, Weatherby worked hard at farm jobs. His early life is a story of hardship during which cardboard was used to cover holes in his shoes and his hunting and fishing were required to supplement the family's meals.

As we have seen repeatedly in our interviews, many of the characteristics that eventually lead to entrepreneurial success are born in the face of obstacles in the entrepreneur's youth. And so it was with Roy Weatherby, who developed his determination and perseverance to achieve at an early age. In fact, his entrepreneurial spirit first surfaced when he earned a Daisy BB gun by selling garden seed. He recalls, "I sold every seed package by walking from neighbor to neighbor, with none living closer than a mile from one another."

In addition, like many entrepreneurs, Roy had vision, drive, and tenacity, but also like many he was constantly trying to make ends meet. The financial problems he faced at various times were often overbearing, distracting him from developing superior ammunition and firearms. Because Weatherby's career was specially dogged by financial hardship (it took 37 years before he owned the entire company, buying out his last partners in 1983), his story provides an opportunity to explore the importance of proper capitalization and financial management to entrepreneur success.

After attending night classes at the University of Wichita for a couple of years, Weatherby worked for Southwestern Bell. In 1937, during the Great Depression, he requested a leave of absence from the telephone company and with his supportive wife, Camilla, moved to southern California where he took an insurance job with the Southern California Automobile Club. He was quite successful in his new career, but his love of ballistics and firearms lured him away from his $600 a month salary (which was a considerable salary in the early 1940's). The decision indicates his capacity to face risks and his confidence in his abilities to make his way in the world.

To subsidize his early ballistics research efforts, he opened a small sporting goods store and, with a $189 Sears lathe and an $89 drill press, he began to transform what was once a hobby into a profession. "I started with no money. At times I had to borrow from friends to meet my little payroll. I was broke before I started but I had ideas, tremendous ambition, tenacity, and I knew I had more than ample determination."

As critical as these characteristics were to Weatherby's eventual success, one key ingredient was missing at the time — capital! In 1946 he sold 50 percent of his company for $10,000 to an attorney aquaintance who enjoyed guns and who was enamored with Weatherby's work.

For the most part, the new capital retired loans, with the balance invested in new machinery and equipment. However, cash flow strains soon resurfaced and the family sold the 160-acre Kansas farm that his wife had inherited. The $21,000 from this sale allowed Weatherby to repurchase the attorney's stock and buy additional equipment for making gun barrels and stocks. The use of cash for fixed assets continued to strain cash flow to the point that payroll checks sometimes bounced. In a final effort, Roy incorporated and decided to issue and sell $75,000 in stock. By Weatherby's admission, he was not a book-keeper. His attorney at the time advised him that he was broke and that there was no way he could sell stock in a company that had a negative net worth.

Weatherby persisted and eventually sold the shares in his newly incorporated company. The new stockholders were impressed with Roy Weatherby. They were investing in the man and his ideas. As his company grew, its financial require-ments expanded, with Weatherby constantly involved in raising capital. It was a game of catch-up and it took its toll. It involved several mergers and eventually resulted in Weatherby finally buying out the last of his partners in 1983, almost four decades after he started the company.

When asked if his objective in starting the company was to make money, he answered, "No, not really, it was simply necessary (to make money) in order for me to pursue my love of guns and ballistics. When I was young, money was a neces-sity and I would take risks because I could always start over. As I grew older, I knew I couldn't start over and I took fewer risks. Today, my son Ed, the president of the company, has many wonderful ideas which included the production of the lesser priced Vanguard models and the Fibermark. But, the financial strain and battles I fought have left their mark and I am more conservative than I once was and not willing to take the same risks."

Independence

Today we see numerous publicly held firms being purchased by management and going private. Financial gains are certainly an important reason for management to pursue a stock repurchase, and in some cases it may be a strategy for avoiding a hostile takeover that may threaten management's very existence at the company. However, there is a third reason for management to purchase the stock, especially for entrepreneurial firms with outside investors. Outside money means outside influence and control. In many cases this is viewed as interference by the entrepreneurial founder/manager, no matter how positive or well-meaning the advice may be.

This interference seems to curtail the individualistic and free spirited entrepreneur and restrict his/her independence, a key entrepreneurial characteristic. With the vital capital that is needed to start the company comes an implied right of the investor to intervene and protect the investment. As the firm matures and expands, the entrepreneur generally experiences increasing pressure from outside investors to share the management of the company. The entrepreneur will also experience increasing self-imposed pressure to regain his/her independence by repurchasing the investors' position, thereby eliminating outside interference.

Both the introduction of new management and the presence of investors are necessary in the maturing of any new company, but they nevertheless tend to hamstring the entrepreneur, who sees himself as moving out of the mainstream of the company's affairs toward a figurehead position. This creates a number of conflicts for the entrepreneur. Psychologically he often feels betrayed, since he views the company as an extension of himself. In addition, he feels stifled because his creativity and individualism are being supressed.

This investor/founder conflict is natural, given that the priorities of the two differ. Investors tend to be conservative by nature with priority on return on investment. The entrepreneur on the other hand, as we have tried to show in this book, is individualistic and free spirited and given to taking risks. The growth of the company eventually creates the need for bureaucracy as investors strive to maximize returns. Bureaucracy, of course, is completely counter to the entrepreneurial spirit, and the investor/founder love-hate syndrome is the inevitable result.

Like many entrepreneurs, Roy Weatherby began his company by performing most of the tasks necessary to run a new business: equipment maintenance, sales, bookkeeping, and marketing among others. As the company grew this became painfully trying.

Weatherby gradually introduced new management to the company, relinquishing many of the duties he regularly performed but regaining some lost independence to work on new product designs.

In the beginning, many of Weatherby's investors were intrigued with the romance associated with firearms. But the romance eventually gave way to the hard facts that Weatherby was involved in capital intensive research and development that constantly required additional financing, which meant constantly finding new investors to replace or supplement existing ones. The cycle was repeated many times, causing tremendous interference with Weatherby's product research and design pursuits and creating endless distractions.

When Weatherby reached the point where he could afford to regain total control of his firm, he did not have the convenience of a stock market to buy out his partners, since the firm was privately held. He had to negotiate with each investor. His experience now leads us to encourage entrepreneurial readers of this book, when soliciting capital for their businesses, to try to establish the procedures for eventually repurchasing an investor's position right at the outset. When the repurchase formula is identified beforehand, ambiguity and potential conflict are avoided later, making it much easier for the entrepreneur to regain his independence later when he has the necessary recources to do so.

Sacrifice Roy Weatherby's story is one of
extreme sacrifice, primarily of his
family. "For all my activity, I shamefully neglected my wife
and my three children because it meant twelve and fifteen-
hour days, almost seven days a week." This sacrifice is borne
emotionally but also philosophically by Weatherby. When
asked if he would do it again and pay the price of family neglect
and financial obstacles, he states with reflection, "I don't really
know because you simply can't know what you don't know;
that insight comes with time."

At seventy-five, Chairman of the Board Weatherby is facing
another obstacle and potential sacrifice, perhaps his greatest
one as an entrepreneur—when and how to relinquish his position and his daily decision making authority. To do this he must
reach into his soul as the person whose qualities created and
inspired the company from the start.

Capital and Financial Weatherby was most candid in our
Management interview and discussed many of
the financial obstacles he had overcome. As we indicated, he
finally gained sole ownership of his company in 1983 after
thirty-seven years of varied and complex financing arrange-
ments. With his permission, we thought it appropriate to
expound on some of the basics of finance in the hope that it
will help other entrepreneurs. If you own your own business
or intend to start one, we strongly recommend that you read
this section carefully.

One may have excellent ideas and all the traits associated
with entrepreneurial success, yet the fact remains that proper
capitalization and financial management are a must. This is
the lifeblood of any successful endeavour, and lack of proper
capital and financial management seems to be the major factor
in the demise of many start-up attempts.

Proper capitalization means sufficient cash to provide
the founders with the funds necessary to produce the pro-

duct and deliver it to market. Initial capital comes from two basic sources: investors (equity) and loan granting institutions (debt), or a combination thereof. Each of these sources of cash have their advantages and disadvantages for the new company.

Investor advantages:

- Provides funds without interest expense, thereby improving cash flow and profitability.

- Usually is not tied to specific terms and conditions, thereby providing flexibility.

- Investors usually understand and accept associated risks without recourse to the founder.

- The investment is usually unsecured, providing additional flexibility. For example, inventory liquidation in response to adversity would normally not be a problem.

Investor disadvantages:

- Results in the dilution of the founder's ownership, sometimes resulting in loss of control.
- Usually requires a return on equity corresponding with the perceived risk. The amount may reach 30-40 percent per year, considerably greater than bank credit.

- Investors have an understandable tendency to minimize risk, resulting in efforts to play a more active role in the company than an institutional lender might. This involvement may reach a point of interference, disrupting the operation, and can make for an unhealthy relationship.

Institutional loan advantages:

- Ownership is retained by the founders.

- Usually can be obtained at a reasonable and relatively stable cost.

- Bankers usually do not want to be involved in the daily operations of the firm. However, the credit questions will be penetrating and may result in some operating constraints to ensure loan repayment and protection of the loan.

Institutional loan disadvantages:

- Often, the lender requires recourse to the founders even if the loan is made to the company.

- Bank loans usually include operating constraints.

- If problems occur, banks may not have the desire or flexibility to stay with the company and the bank may elect to call the loan.

In sum, investors have a tendency to be more involved in the company and expect a larger risk return. However, their positions usually are unsecured and they tend to be more empathetic in the face of adversity, compared to institutional lenders who tend to be more bureaucratic when troubles arise, particularly if attorneys are involved in the matter. On the other hand, bank credit requires periodic interest payments, which reduces cash flow, and usually involves security with recourse to the founder's personal assets. But, banks usually do not take ownership in the firm. Naturally there are exceptions to these rules and many institutional lenders actively participate in some forms of ownership, especially in leverage buyouts where they can increase their yields. But for a start-up operation, banks rarely take an equity position.

Banks prefer not to loan money if the amount of debt will exceed the company's net worth. It is usual, therefore, for founders to first obtain investor funds and then, when the company's operations can support it, to seek bank credit. So even if bank credit is involved it will first require investor equity in the form of a cash investment or a guarantee of the bank debt in the event the loan cannot be repaid.

Obtaining capital will require a well thought out game plan to induce outside individuals to risk cash. The plan should be comprehensive and not only discuss the product and the unique characteristics of the industry, but it should also thoroughly explore the downside risks and identify contingency plans for coping with various potential problems.

This planning process is a critical discipline.It is arduous and often new to the entrepreneur. However, a well conceived plan will demonstrate credibility to outsiders (investors, bankers and suppliers) and should become an integral part of the corporate culture. The plan should be dynamic and on-going, not a once-a-year process to pacify creditors or investors. It should focus on objectives and strategies for achievement, assess the environmental influences impacting the plan, and identify capabilities in light of objectives. This discipline forms the foundation for the corporate radar and action plan and limits the knee-jerk reaction mentality that is far too common and and often leads to the collapse of even large and well-established firms.

Integral to the planning process is proper financial management. Financial statements are a reflection of management's past actions and decisions. They are the record of judgment against which lenders, investors, and management can view the progress of the firm.

We reemphasize that the greatest threat to the entrepreneurial effort is lack of proper capitalization and poor financial controls and management. This is primarily due to the entrepreneur's general lack of financial insight and his focus on his pet product or service at the expense of financial matters. Too often the entrepreneur dumps this aspect of his job in the bookkeeper's lap or hands it off to the accountant. But this doesn't work, because these professionals record what has happened, they do not participate in planning the future.

Roy Weatherby's Thoughts to Entrepreneurship

We respected the privacy of all our interviewees by providing them with our draft of their interviews for their review and incorporating their changes. The following are excerpts from Mr. Weatherby's review of his chapter:

1) As he goes along, the entrepreneur learns every phase of the operation, and has all or most of the answers. Delegating responsibility is very difficult until a business has grown enough to hire specialists that can be trained. I think this is one of the great mistakes that a lot of entrepreneurs, as well as young presidents, make, feeling they can delegate all of their work to someone else. Even today, there is a tremendous amount of my work that I cannot delegate. I have to do it myself. When you start out as an entrepreneur, you are building a business, and in my case, it was around a particular name, so I handled a great deal of correpondence. And yet today, when some unhappy or happy dealer writes me, I answer the letter. Certainly, it could be delegated, but when you get a personal reply thanking you, it means a great deal. When you receive a letter from the President of the United States, it makes one realize that the founder of any company has to be accessible to the public. That is all part of good, solid, valuable promotion, and as it stands today, I delegate everything possible for me to delegate without hurting the company. I do have a few people to whom I can delegate some of the more technical and serious work, but only a very few. I don't think that any entrepreneur will ever be successful if he feels he can just start out delegating.

2) I have read quite a bit of Peter Drucker's writing and I read an interview with Drucker the other day that was interesting, but don't agree with some of Drucker's theories about entrepreneurial success. He mentioned entrepreneurs as being "gifted" and that I agree with. A lot of people are gifted with something. Discipline is an

absolute must. He indicated you could become an entrepreneur by properly disciplining yourself but I don't agree
with that. You must dicipline yourself, but if you don't
have the abilities—the inherited abilities—disciplining
yourself is not enough. Of course, there are other kinds
of entrepreneurs; those who have gone to work with large
companies, learned the phase of their business thoroughly,
and retired early to start in business for themselves. It is
difficult but it is so much easier than starting without the
knowledge or the money.

3) I agree that proper capitalization and financial management are "musts." But a person is able, I believe, to become
an entrepreneur if he has the abilities to learn from his
mistakes and to sell people on the idea of investing capital.
But if he can't do that, he will never be any more than
a one man show because it certainly takes capital and
financial management, as well as good general management
and many sacrifices. I had to learn the hard way that I
needed cash forecasts. I had to figure out what my antici-
pated sales were going to be, and everything I had to
pay out, to see what I might have left over so I would
know months in advance whether I was going to have any
money for any type of advancement or even to take care
of payables.

4) Regarding institutional loan advantages, of course in my
case, there was no possibility of obtaining a loan and loans
are very dangerous. The bank can close you down at any
time. In fact, in the early days, I couldn't even borrow
money from the loan sharks that charged double interest.
However, today, we have a very fine relationship with the
Bank of America and have a substantial line of credit, but
no one should ever get to feeling too secure because the
minute your financial statements begin to go the other
direction, you will find the bank is no longer a friend
of yours. As the old saying goes, you can borrow the
umbrella when it isn't raining, but before you can obtain

an unsecured loan, you really have to have a considerable amount of net worth.

5) I think that overoptimism plays a great part in the failure of many entrepreneurial ventures. In my earlier days, because of my lack of practical experience, I really didn't know what I could or couldn't do. I didn't realize how closely you had to watch expenditures and obligations. Generally speaking, there are an awful lot of entrepreneurs that start out without the formal education that is necessary, such as business administration, accounting, and management. So many of them have to learn the hard and expensive way and a great number of them flounder before they get going. Of course, you [the author] are saying the same thing, but in different words. And you are certainly right when you say being able to build a successful product and give good service doesn't necessarily mean success. You have to have the financing, as well as good financial and general managers. They are available, but when you don't have any money, you can't hire them, so you have to muddle through the best you can.

6) As I go through all of these pages that you have written on the subject, it gives me a rather sick feeling. It makes me remember yesterday. Then I ask myself, would you do it all over again? I believe if I had known what I would have to go through to get where I am, I am not sure I would have ever started in the first place, but that is how people get started; they are young, inexperienced, and they don't know; they can't see what they are getting into and then they get in deeper and deeper and finally have passed the no return mark.

Epilogue

Roy Weatherby's career was battered by financial hardship. By his own gracious and humble admission, "It took its toll, for the only bad times and regrets were caused by finiancial problems, nothing else."

The fact that Weatherby prevailed and other entrepreneurs often do not is due to his preserverance in overcoming obstacles, primarily financial hurdles.*

After our interview with Roy Weatherby, he successfully sold his company to his son and daughters and the legend lives on with Ed Weatherby as the new Chief Executive Officer.

*For additional information on the subject of finance, see Bill MacPhee, *Short-Term Business Borrowings* (Dow-Jones-Irwin, 1984).

Chapter 13

Forrest and Nina Wood of Ranger Boats

Forrest and Nina Wood of Ranger Boats

"A Consumer-Driven Family Culture"

*N*estled in the foothills of the beautiful Ozark Mountains is Flippin, Arkansas, home of Ranger Boats, a company that employs 460 of Flippin's 1,000 residents. Forrest and Nina Wood are the founders of Wood Manufacturing Inc., builder of the famous Ranger Boat, the leading bass fishing boat in terms of sales, safety, efficiency, comfort, and hull design. Selling for between $10,000 and $25,000, Ranger Boats are handmade, employing state-of-the-art, NASA-designed materials and high-tech electronics for navigation and fish location. These boats are powered by a variety of engines and are capable of exceeding speeds of sixty miles per hour, enabling fishermen to quickly and safely cover large bodies of water in pursuit of fish or for protection in the event of storms.

The Woods do not employ engineers but prefer to rely on their employees who fish, on tournament fishermen and consumers, and on their wealth of common sense for boat design. As Forrest states, "Ranger Boats are designed by fishermen, built by fishermen, for fishermen. Although we build boats, we sell reliable pleasure for our customers and we care about our product. We service customers both before and after the sale because *they are* the Ranger family!"

Because of the small size of the community it's located

in, Wood Manufacturing provides a rare opportunity to view corporate culture in a relatively controlled environment. In the remainder of this chapter, we will explore the values, rituals, and heroes that make this organization's style the envy of many large American corporations that continue to struggle in vain for identity, purpose, and market share.

Background

Both Forrest and Nina were born in 1932, and raised in Marion County, Arkansas. Their families were farmers. Their fathers had other jobs to subsidize the farm income, leaving Forrest and Nina to take on responsibilities far beyond those generally assumed by children. Both took part in the hard work of growing cotton and corn and raising cattle while going to school. They learned the meaning of sacrifice at a young age. Nina and her mother chopped wood for two new school dresses when she was thirteen, while at the same age Forrest was cutting, hauling, and stacking hay, a tedious and backbreaking job. Forrest always wanted to be "a grown-up," as his father recounts, "Forrest was never a boy; he was born a young man and he took responsibility quickly."

Forrest was always aggressive about whatever he pursued; he wanted to accomplish things immediately but also thoroughly. Before modern hay bailing and loading equipment, the primary collection method was to load hay onto wagons and unload it by hand. Forrest's inclination to "get on with the job" was (and is) an impelling creative force. Frustrated by this time-consuming way of bailing and loading, he devised a method whereby two ropes were lain diagonally along the wagon bed, onto which he would stack the hay. He would detach the horses and move them to the side of the wagon and bring the ropes from the opposite side, over the hay, and tie them to the horses. The horses would pull the ropes thereby unloading the hay, which was considerably faster than unloading with a pitch fork. This kind of creative efficiency has been a trademark of Forrest's career.

Forrest graduated from high school in 1950 and in 1951 he married Nina Kirkland. He had saved his money to buy cattle and his "get on with the job" attitude led him to forming a joint venture with a financial backer to borrow money to raise cattle. That year, his area of the country experienced a severe drought and cattle feed was scarce. Trusting Forrest's judgement and integrity, which were by then well established in Marion County, the partner agreed to take on feeding the cattle for another year. During this time, Forrest added to his farm duties by working nights as a laborer on the Bull Shoals Dam, hauling rock and concrete and digging dynamite holes.

After the second year, the cattle were sold, but the resultant income was insufficient to retire the loan. Raised with a deep feeling of obligation to repay the cattle debt, Forrest and Nina moved to Kansas City, Missouri, where he took a job at an aircraft plant, assembling F-84 fighter planes for the Korean War effort. They were young and Kansas City was a big city to them. Although lonely they met their obligations, and repaid the debt. During that time, Forrest became a skilled laborer, which would serve him well in the future years.

Within two years, two of their four daughters were born. In addition to repaying the debt they were able to buy some land back in Marion County to farm corn, hay, and raise cattle, their first love. Forrest recounts, "I appreciated the opportunity to work [in Kansas City] because I had a big debt to repay, and I learned a lot about quality construction. However, I yearned to be my own boss, and it got to a point where the worst thing life could give me was a good job, so we returned to Arkansas."

By the age of twenty, Forrest and Nina had clearly demonstrated their propensity for hardwork, sacrifice, and integrity.

A Sense of Quality

While farming and raising cattle, Forrest and Nina continued to pursue other income opportunities to supplement their farm income. They had always enjoyed fishing and the Bull Shoals

Dam had created superb trout fishing streams in the area, as well as some of the finest bass fishing in the country. Seizing the opportunity, they got into the float trip business. "We started with three or four flat bottom Jon boats and I would hire out as a guide. The word got around that we provided a good outing and the business expanded to the point where we bought more boats and hired more guides. I learned that people would pay a premium for top quality and that a man would part with his money for a good time faster than if he were negotiating for the necessities. We provided the very best guide service, equipment, fishing, and food. We didn't just slap cheese between two pieces of bread; Nina and the girls baked pork chops and fried chicken, and we always had some homemade pies." This attention to quality and customer service became and remains to this day the foundation of Ranger Boats, where the boats are sold at a premium but where quality, safety, comfort, and service are never compromised.

The float trips also revealed another theme that prevails at Ranger Boats today; the business was a collective enterprise, with Nina, Forrest, and their four daughters Rhonda, Brenda, Donna, and Linda all participating. "The girls had farm chores when the cooking was done for the float trips at 5:00 a.m., and after school. We relied on each other the way you do in farming. I think the farm life gives you just a little something in life that others don't have: an appreciation for getting the job done and for self-sufficiency. I don't tell my people what to do at Ranger—if they see a job undone, they do it." The Woods built a top quality guide service over fourteen years, recognizing that by providing the best they would develop the best clientele and encourage repeat business.

The float business is seasonal and the Woods had a good crew who needed employment, as did Forrest, in the long off-season, so Forrest entered the construction business. His guides became construction workers and together they built everything from houses to bridges. Forrest's experience on Bull Shoals Dam, in road construction and carpentry, and at building planes provided the knowledge for their construction efforts. His eye for quality and detail gave him a reputation as a top quality contractor. "Even today I go up to a house I built twenty years ago to check out the cornices; they're straight! A person should expect quality and value and if you can't give it, then don't do it because it's really easier to do it right the first time."

On occasion Forrest would barely break even on a construction job in order to build the best and to incorporate changes he believed necessary that were discovered after the price was set; a refreshing attitude that contrasts sharply with business approaches that rely on cost overruns. "I built a house for a man and called to get his thoughts on something. He just told me to do what I thought was best. Well, it turned out that what I thought was best nearly lost me money on the job."

In the early 1960's, Forrest was hired by a group of Houston developers to build a bridge twenty feet wide and sixty feet long over a gorge. "The slope was so steep we couldn't get a bulldozer down to the creek bottom so we tied chains around the boulders and pulled the rocks out of the canyon. It was the hardest work I had ever done. The locals said the bridge would never stand the floods, but we put down a good footing and with a hand mixer and our country boy ways, we poured the base and laid the top. I still drive over that bridge and it gives me a good feeling of a job well done, just like I get a bubble in my throat when I pass a Ranger Boat on the highway; I know that it's a job well done!" This story reveals an important aspect of Forrest and Nina: they work with their people and they have never asked a person to do something they haven't at one time done themselves. This has brought them the uncompromising respect and loyalty of the Ranger family.

By 1966 the Woods had established a successful float trip business, they had an enviable construction operation, and in their "spare time" farmed and raised cattle. At this time some bass fishing boats were being built, but the industry was very much in its infancy. Forrest was just beginning to lay fiberglass over flat Jon boats and had already hired a fiber-glass man and two helpers. Bass fishing tournaments were beginning to spring up. Forrest saw an opportunity and decided to become serious about building bass fishing boats. When their first boat was finished and ready for the water test, Forrest arrived from one of his construction jobs to find his three boat builders looking forlorn. After they put the boat back in the water, he quickly understood why they were so chagrined. "The boat ran with its nose in the water." In traditional Wood spirit, Forrest said, "Well, let's find out the problem," and they began experimenting and securing 2 x 4's at various positions and angles and eventually got the modified Jon boat to trim properly.

Opportunistic as to Luck and Timing

That year, a bass tournament was held on Greers Ferry, a local lake, where Forrest introduced his odd looking Jon boat with the high powered name of "Ranger." "I liked the name because it commanded respect, like the Texas Rangers, whose stories tell of uncompromising pursuit of their prey." Forrest left the tournament with four boat orders in hand, and thus Ranger Boats was born.

In 1968, Ray Scott, the promoter and driving force behind the Bass Master Classic (world champion tournament) was hold-ing his first championship. Forrest went to the Alabama tour-nament with his Ranger boat and returned to Flippin with six more boat orders scribbled on paper napkins. More importantly, this trip began the long and intimate relationship between Ranger Boats and the Bass Master Classic, and the development of one of the youngest and fastest growing industries in the U.S., bass fishing, which has now achieved multi-billion-dollar sales.

Forrest realized that professional fishermen would provide ideas and requirements that should be incorporated in his boats. What was once a flat bottom fiberglass Jon boat was evolving into a functional fishing machine with tackle box holders, rod containers, holding tanks with aerators to keep fish alive for conservation purposes, and other innovative features. "The bass tournaments are to fishing what the Indy 500 and Sebring were to the development of the auto industry, where the product was put under the most severe tests. We didn't go to the tournaments just to sell boats, but to learn about our products, consumers' needs, and to incorporate the changes."

As the volume of business began to increase, in 1969, Forrest and Nina leased an old wooden building with 10,000 square feet of floor space and moved the young boat business from their barn to the deserted Silver Star dance hall. Although the boats were well built, incorporating many of the changes proposed by professional tournament fishermen, the new business initially lost money. "I guess that's the evolution of any business, you lose a little money until you understand the nature of the business." But it forced them into making a decision concerning their various business interests: float trips, construction, farming, and boats.

Construction gave way to boats, and Forrest began dedicating himself to building the Ranger tradition. Forrest and Nina saw the potential for top quality fishing boats, and they felt that Ray Scott, with his sophisticated promotional ability, would succeed in expanding the industry. With entrepreneurial vision and self-confidence they sacrificed a sound construction business to pursue a new and exciting venture, with all its unknowns. "Who would have ever guessed that fifteen years later we would be producing 4,000 boats a year with 800 orders chasing our production schedule."

Ability to Overcome Obstacles

Shortly after Forrest began devoting attention to the boat business, the company began making money. As always, Forrest was capitalizing his own labor and sacrificing personal income for the long haul. In May 1971, the business was well underway, with

Forrest at the helm and Nina, stride-for-stride, keeping the books and managing the office. On May 4, 1971, Forrest and Nina were hosting Roland Martin, the all time bass tournament money winner, for dinner when they heard the Flippin fire bell. Concerned for their neighbors and community, they loaded in a pick-up to find the fire and help the fire fighters. Rushing through the countryside, they crested the velvet green hills of Flippin to see the most explosive fire in the history of Marion County — *Ranger Boats was in flames*!

They approached the fire in silence and disbelief, watching enormous flames erupt from the volatile plastics and explosive acetone. Forrest recounts, "You know, that fire tested my priorities, and our first thought was for our night crew, not for our business, which was uninsured." After checking his people, Forrest rushed to the inferno, kicked open a window and dragged a desk to the wall, salvaging sixty boat orders from the U.S. Navy. He then tried to enter the gutted dance hall, but a fireman restrained him as the roof collapsed. The community of Flippin had gathered to watch the demise of Ranger Boats. Some employees spoke of collecting unemployment and planting a garden, seeing their careers go up in smoke, with all being quite confident that Ranger was dead and that the economic foundation of Flippin was gone.

With his sixty boat orders in hand, Forrest saw a farmer friend in the crowd and said, "If you still have that old Ford tractor at your place, I believe I'll need it tomorrow to start cleaning the ashes so we can build these sixty boats." That evening Forrest and Nina talked into the night, and they emerged the next morning with faith in their people at Ranger, in their dealers, and in their customers that Ranger could be revived.

The morning after the fire Forrest had a telephone nailed to a tree and Rhonda, his daughter, had her first job answering the telephone for boat orders as Forrest cleared the rubble. Not only did boat orders continue, but many dealers called offering advance payment on their boats to finance the rebuilding effort. This emotional display of confidence in Forrest,

Nina, and Ranger Boats reaffirmed their determination to "get on with the job." Nina recalls, "forty days and forty nights after the $150,000 fire, a new metal building was erected and Ranger had a new home." During the reconstruction period, an old friend offered his machine shop, where they were able to build boats, and the sixty salvaged boat orders were met *on time*!

To rebuild their plant, Forrest and Nina approached the Small Business Administration (SBA) for a loan. The SBA was encouraging, but the approval process was too long. To expedite the process they went to a local bank, which loaned the money but required $4 collateral for every $1 loaned, an exorbitant ratio of debt to security. Over the years, Forrest and Nina had invested their income from their profitable float trip and construction businesses in land and cattle; the collateral was there, and they literally "bet the farm" on the rebirth of Ranger Boats. However, working capital was still short, so after fourteen years in business, they made a major, heartbreaking decision to sell their profitable and hard built float trip company. "You know, the bank didn't treat us very well with the huge collateral they required. Unknown to the bank, it did us a real favor because we became even more efficient in order to service the loan and get back our property, which we did. I realized later, after owning some bank stock, how naive they were when we had the sixty boat orders from the Navy, which they agreed to pay for within thirty days of delivery, and the bank still nearly didn't make the loan. I don't think they ever stopped to realize that the survival of Ranger meant the successful repayment of a lot of loans made to the locals working at Ranger."

As if to test the conviction and tenacity of the Wood family, nature struck a second blow to Marion County in 1971. Six months after the fire, a tornado ripped through Flippin, causing tremendous damage. As it struck, Forrest and Nina rushed their four daughters to the ground shelter, but the tornado slammed into their house before they got to the refuge. Grabbing the children, the Wood's threw them to the floor and covered them with their bodies for protection. "If you haven't been in a tornado, let me tell you it will get your undivided attention. It's like laying between two freight trains passing each other at eighty miles an hour." The wind destroyed a newly painted barn, scattering hay for miles; it tore the roof off of the house, and slung a horse trailer a quarter of a mile, leaving it nesting in a tree.

After checking their daughters, the Woods did what they always do in emergencies, they loaded in the pick-up and searched Marion County for friends and family and helped with emergency clean-up. During the night, the Woods were totally involved with their community. It wasn't until morning light that they realized that their own property had sustained the worst damage from the tornado.

Sacrifice

"I don't think many people fully appreciate the sacrifices of an entrepreneur. They appreciate the money and recognition, but I don't think they realize the responsibility, sacrifice, and loneliness that goes with it; it can be enormous." Forrest and Nina sacrificed their private time and sleep. Working seven days a week, they routinely put in fifteen-to-eighteen-hour days. After the fire, they built boats during the day, and Forrest often returned home late at night to shower, change, and drive all night delivering boats to dealers. "During one week, I noted my sleep time; from Tuesday morning to Saturday I had twenty hours of sleep." In the early years Nina stayed with their daughters until they graduated from high school while Forrest traveled selling and delivering boats.

When home, the Woods personally performed every aspect of building their boats, and a number of their employees recount, "They are hard workers, but they would never ask someone to do something they haven't done." This demonstration of hard work and sacrifice earned the Woods the respect and dedication of their people. "If Forest ever saw you just standing around, he would simply start working on your job; he wouldn't say anything; he didn't have to."

This sacrifice of private time was put to the test when Forrest realized his daughters were growing up while his time was devoted to farming and building boats. "Life is a balancing act, and I realized that life with my family was passing me by. What saved our family was the tornado — it made us all more appreciative of life, each other, and our family. Sometimes you nearly lose something before you fully appreciate it."

The entire Wood family enjoys cattle and horses. This appreciation taught the girls responsibility at an early age. "When our daughters were teenagers they had jobs, and if they wanted a horse they took care of it along with their other farming chores, they were not down at the soda shop." Forrest and Nina encouraged their daughters' interest in horses, and they began traveling to numerous horse shows and competitions. "Many nights I would return from delivering boats, early in the morning. I would change clothes, load the girls' horses, and off we went to a horse show."

This sacrifice is remembered vividly by the girls and the employees, as one stated, "I really don't know how the Woods did it, but I sure respect their family and community devotion." Their personal sacrifices for the company and family earned Nina and Forrest the utmost respect from their people, who often sacrifice "in order to get the job done." Forrest and Nina recount the many times their people stayed well after closing time to get boats ready for delivery, or came in on the weekend, sacrificing their time to finish the job. "I don't have to tell my people we're all in this together; they're self-motivated and they work together for the common good of the Ranger family. You don't get the respect of your people simply by signing the paycheck; they earned that; you get their respect through earning it by your own conduct."

The ability to sacrifice is a primary trait of the entrepreneur, whose personal pleasures are often foresaken in exchange for long-term success. The independence of being one's own boss gives way to the responsibility of guiding the organization, its future, and its people. "It's a tremendous responsibility for your people, your dealers, and your customers—you're really never independent of your responsibility, you're only independent in that you have choices. It can be very lonesome struggling with those choices and realizing the impact if you're wrong.''

Promotional Skills   The Ranger promotional philosophy was not spawned at Harvard or Stanford; it evolved from Forrest's and Nina's common sense. ''Proper marketing begins with building the very best product to satisfy a need, making people aware that you have the product, and then treating the consumer right after the sale.'' At Ranger, the best materials that go into making the boats are purchased; quality begins with quality ingredients. Raw materials are often picked up and delivered to Flippin by Ranger boat delivery trucks after they deliver boats to customers. This reduces shipping costs, increases truck utilization, and improves trailer maintenance, since an empty trailer sustains greater strain than a loaded one. The boat trailers and delivery trailers, by the way, also are made by Wood.

The Ranger promotional philosophy begins with its leaders, Forrest and Nina, who attend numerous bass fishing tournaments and provide products as awards for tournament winners. Forrest is an active bass contender himself.

Since 1971, Ranger has provided the boat awards for the Bass Master Classic, the world series of bass fishing. Fully rigged, these boats retail for $20,000, and are outfitted with state-of-the-art navigation and fish-locating electronics. The contest boats are outfitted by Ranger, rather than by dealers which is customary. This allows Ranger to see first-hand what problems dealers run into in outfitting their boats, which has led to numerous changes in the boat design resulting in improvements in the quality of the Ranger-dealer relationship.

Forrest is an active participant in the bass tournaments, and has qualified for two of the Bass Master Classics. This is a rigorous effort, with contestants earning points based on pounds of fish caught at various tournaments. The top thirty contenders compete for the World Champion title, with cash prizes and a new Ranger boat awarded. In one ironic burst of fate occurred in 1979 when Forrest was competing in the New York Invitational Bass Tournament. As the competition came to a close, Forrest and Bobby Murray were head-to-head. In the end, Forrest won with 46.5 pounds of bass caught over two days, beating Bobby, the two time World Champion, by six ounces. "Bobby's an excellent fishermen but I guess it wasn't meant to be for him that day and *I won a Ranger boat!*"

From the beginning, the Bass Master Classic has been held at an undisclosed location to prevent the contestants from studying the lake and to more truly test their knowledge of fish habitat and behavior. In providing the boats for the contestants, Ranger truck drivers have no idea of their eventual destination as they zigzag across the country on what appears each year to be a truck convoy on a scavanger hunt. In one of the years Forrest Wood qualified for the Bass Master Classic, to ensure that he had no knowledge of the location of the tournament (since he was providing the boats), he voluntarily surrendered himself to the sheriff at the Memphis Bass Club and was incarcerated in the Memphis jail until the thirty contestants met, boarded a chartered plane, and, while *en route,* learned of their destination. In recalling the experience Forrest states, "I must admit that I had better than usual accommodations."

These tournaments are vitally important for Ranger. They promote the product by associating it with the top professional tournament fishermen, while putting the boats through the most grueling punishment. The tourrnaments provide Wood with the opportunity to learn first hand of the fishermen's needs, which are often incorporated in new boat design. Ranger Boats has evolved in and through this intimate relationship between the Woods and the fishermen; no other chief executive of a boat compeny is as visable or as involved with the sport as Forrest and Nina Wood are.

Tournament fishermen and other fishing gear consumers respect and identify with Forrest. "He's one of us and he listens to our needs." In addition, Nina, an avid and accomplished fisherwoman in her own right, often attends the tournaments and takes pictures of the contestants and often sends prints to the fishermen, regardless of the boat they're using, another personal Wood touch that adds to the industry-wide respect they hold.

While preparing for the Wood chapter, this author asked a tournament fisherman who represents another boat company, "Who builds the best fishing boat?" The competitor didn't balk, stating, "Forrest and Nina Wood build the best, the safest, and the most efficient fishing machine!" A competitor recounts, "Forrest is a tough competitor but as we're idling in the staging area waiting our turn to go for the fish, he'll throttle over and ask my opinion on something regarding the Ranger."

Customer and Supplier Loyalty

Since Forrest, Nina, and their employees all fish, they are constantly coming up with changes, modifications, and improvements that are incorporated in Ranger boats. "We are in touch and keep our hand on the consumer's pulse! When was the last time Iacocca drove a car at Indy?" beams a Ranger employee. "We know that what's good for the industry is good for Ranger."

Forrest states, "We are consumer-driven and we build our boats against dealer orders, no spec boats." Ranger's dealer relationships are carefully nurtured. Parts are usually shipped within twenty-four hours of request, and when unique problems arise, Forrest dispatches a technician. "We want the problem solved for customer satisfaction and to incorporate necessary changes in our boats to avoid similar problems. Remember, our customer works hard for his money and in his free time he deserves a boat that is consistently reliable."

In late 1970's the recession affected all companies, but the boat industry was especially hard hit. At the time, Ranger was running two full-page color ads in BASS magazine. Ray Scott, the editor of the publication, called Forrest and said, "I know times are tough and you certainly won't hurt my feelings if you drop one of your ads in my magazine." Forrest replied, "Let's take out a third ad." Forrest and Nina feel a deep responsibility and loyalty to their dealers and customers. "When times are tough, our dealers and customers, which are the Ranger family, need to know that we will be there and that we will deliver the best product and the best service all the time."

The attention to quality and service is complemented by the Woods' attention to safety. The Ranger boat has many safety features. Aside from quality construction, the boats are aerodynamically designed, since most of the hull is airborne at high speed. The boats incorporate kill switches which stop the engine if the driver is thrown from the boat, which tragically occurred to a friend of this author in 1978, resulting in his drowning as the boat sped off.

Ranger boats are designed to stay afloat, a critical safety feature incorporated by the Woods well before it became a Coast Guard requirement. In fact, once when a Ranger boat was stolen and the parts scavenged and sold, to hide the evidence, the culprits removed the drain plug and filled the hull with water; but it floated! Undaunted, they loaded the Ranger with boulders to sink it and left the scene. The following day the sheriff called the boat owner and reported that his Ranger was spotted floating full of boulders, in the lake. Impressed with the Ranger's safety and durability, the owner refurbished the boat and his 1971 Ranger is still in service.

Stories of Rangers' performance are their best promotion. In 1981 Mike Moore, of Little Rock, Arkansas, was fishing the difficult waters of Lake Gurrero, Mexico, when a savage storm broke. Navigating his Ranger in six-to-ten-foot swells, Mike spotted two men clinging to gas cans after their boat had sunk. He rescued the two and all made it safely to shore. One of the two men saved by Mike and his Ranger happened to be Mexico's Finance Minister.

While reviewing this chapter with Forrest and Nina, the following letter from Mr. Don Finwall, who was rescued by a Ranger boat, was received by Forrest:

Dear Mr. Wood,

I've seen your advertisments many times on your Ranger Boats and their safety features, especially "FLOTATION." I've just come home from the West Coast after participating in a two-day Lake Mead fishing tournament, and I am a little lucky to be here. The second day started out good, a little wind, but not bad. But that did change in a hurry. My partner, Tom Mudd, and I started back from the Muddy River area in the Overton Arm into a pretty strong wind, but it was OK, we could handle it. Then we made a right turn at the Overton Beach and all hell broke loose. We had to shut it down off plane and just ride the rollers in. We tried to get to Echo Bay but never made it as we took a wave over the engine and that killed it.

We had no power, I tried to restart the motor for at least a half hour. I put in a new set of spark plugs (which was pretty exciting), but we could not restart the motor. Then out in the middle of the Overton Arm came a 390 Ranger with one Mr. Gary Robson and Mr. Audie Towery to save the day for us. We put a rope (nylon) from his 390 Ranger to the bow of my Avenger and started to Echo Bay. I had both bilge pumps going, but we were taking on more water than we were getting rid of.

I told Tom that if Gary stops we were going in; Gary never stopped but the rope broke; the boat turned over, but we got out. Gary turned around right away and picked Tom and myself up; the four of us watched for about a minute as my boat and every good bait (secret) I owned took a dive. We were able to save nothing but ourselves, thanks to Gary and Audie. You should be very proud of your Ranger people. It's people like Gary Robson and Audie Towery that make me glad to be a small part of it. I can't say enough about how unselfish these two men were to risk their own necks and equipment to help us. A very, very big thanks to them from our two families. And you can bet your last hat, that the next boat I buy will be full of flotation. You don't know how hard it was to watch everything you had of value go down in 250 feet of water, but the last word is, we are here to start over. Thanks once more to the Ranger people.

Sincerely,
Don Finwall
San Fernando, California

Don Finwall ordered a new Ranger in June 1986.

According to Forrest, "The name 'Ranger' stands for reliability in pursuit of the prey. For us it's a symbol that we are proud of and responsible for maintaining, and the product promotes itself. As the story goes, when a riot occurred, the sheriff called for the Texas Rangers. One showed up! The Sheriff asked, 'Where are the other Rangers?' The Ranger said, 'You've got one riot you only need one Ranger.'"

While filming a commercial, Forrest became self-conscious about his "hillbilly" accent and mentioned to the director that he felt he should take voice lessons for future commercials. The director replied, "Oh, I don't think I'd change a thing because you sound believable." There is a genuine quality of sincerity and credibility to Forrest and Nina Wood. And this credibility and sincerity forms the basis, the fundamental message for their successful their efforts at promoting Ranger.

Corporate Culture

The Ranger story shows a remarkable and totally ingenious relationship between Forrest and Nina, their people, consumers, and the industry they helped to develop and continue to nourish. They clearly recognize that an investment in the industry is an investment in Ranger. Unobstructed by bureaucracy, other large employers or a large population and the related social pressures that creates, the Ranger-Flippin community is able to share many of the same values, rituals, traditions and heroes.

In their book *Corporate Cultures* (Addison Wesley, 1982), Deal and Kennedy reveal the results of their study of the relationship between performance and culture. Developing profiles of eighty companies, they found that twenty-five had clearly articulated beliefs. Of the twenty-five, eighteen had qualitative statements such as "IBM means service." These same eighteen companies uniformly were outstanding performers. Ranger's values are summed up in the statement "Ranger Boats are still built one at a time by fishermen, tested by fishermen, for fishermen."

This uncompromising statement serves as a rallying point for employees and consumers. It speaks of a dedication to quality, detail, and understanding of consumer needs and welcomes the consumer to the Ranger family tradition of hard work, hard play, and discipline.

These values are endemic almost to the entire Flippin population. As part of a small farming community, Flippin residents, from birth, are imbued with the values attendant upon hard work, dedication to family and community spirit, appreciation for a "job well done," and a feeling of self-sufficiency. Ranger, an institution bred of the same stock, as our earlier discussion of the Woods would indicate, conveys these very same values.

At Ranger, there is a feeling of equality and an appreciation for interdependence, with each person sensitive to his or her performance as it relates to the final outcome. The absence of a self-serving bureaucracy and the small size of the work force encourage cooperation. One worker stated, "At Ranger, we come to work." It's a statement of exhilaration, contribution, and acknowledged performance of a collective effort, with meaningless titles giving way to a family spirit of a "job well done with pride." A worker sums it up this way, "When I see a Ranger boat, I know my part in the building of that boat, and I get a lump in my throat because I know the owner is driving the best boat made and that he will be comfortable, safe, and proud." Such cultures inspire employee loyalty and at Ranger, twenty of the original thirty employees are still there after fifteen years.

While preparing for this chapter, the author entered the Arkansas Bass Championship. During the grueling two-day tournament we covered approximately 136 miles in a Ranger boat and fished a total of thirty-six hours. In the evenings the pride of the fishermen showed in the stories they loved to tell, an historically rich tradition. The classical irony was that there were more stories about fish than there were fish caught. At the end of the contest, Forrest stood on a houseboat to greet personally the exhausted contestants as they returned to release and weigh their fish.

In that tournament, by the way, there were approximately 126 boats, 78 of which were Rangers. In the finals, seven of the ten contestants were driving Ranger boats.

The values of pride, hard work, and family spirit are the underpinnings of the Ranger culture, and the peer group reinforces these values. If a boat reaches a work station with incomplete or sloppy work, the employee doesn't go to Forrest or Nina, he or she goes directly to the person responsible for the problem. "We're pretty small, and we all know each other outside of Ranger; if you don't perform, everyone knows it." Understanding these values, Forrest and Nina have hired people who exhibited this zeal even if work was not immediately available for them. "In the early days we hired people we knew appreciated a job well done. We were just getting by then, and often we really didn't have a spot for them, but we knew we eventually would." People in advertising, farming, insurance, and other fields were hired and found a spot at Ranger, building boats.

Forrest and Nina's vision has guided the company and they have shaped its values through their leadership and conduct. One of their people states, "Forrest and Nina are the same at Ranger, on the ranch, or at their home, and they have always been that way. You can really count on them; they are steady and reliable. When I make a decision, I always ask if it's one Forrest and Nina would make; they serve as a reference point for us both on and off the job."

Ranger corporate values are reinforced by certain informal

rituals. These rituals are the symbolic cement that reinforces, supports, and sustains its culture.

During the time we spent at Ranger we observed a number of these rituals that captured the Ranger family spirit. Most are informal. Appreciation for a job well done is recognized by a gift commemorating five, ten, and fifteen-year performance. At five years the person receives a Seiko watch, at ten years he or she receives a gold ring with the name 'Ranger' engraved on it and at fifteen years a diamond is added to the ring. One employee remarks, "You couldn't get this ring off my hand, it represents my soul."

Other rituals include company bass fishing tournaments where the employees not only compete, but are provided the opportunity to use the product as it's intended. Forrest states, "At Ranger we work hard and play hard together."

In the spring, the Woods harvest 30,000 bales of hay for their cattle operation. Often Ranger employees will leave the boat factory at the end of their shift and help with the hay harvest — this ritual is indicative of the deep rooted values of both Ranger and Flippin.

Strong corporate cultures like other cultures, also have heroes and Ranger is no exception. As one of the employees stated, "There are a lot of boat companies, some are real good and strong competitors, but we have something nobody has, we have Forrest and Nina Wood."

As Deal and Kennedy note, "If values are the soul of the culture (reinforced by rituals) then heroes personify those values and epitomize the strength of the organization. Heroes are pivotal figures in a strong culture. He is the great motivator, the magnetism, the person everyone will count on when times get tough. They have unshakable character and style. They do things everyone else wants to do but is afraid to try. Heroes are symbolic figures. . . they show that the idea of success lies within the human capacity."

Through their accomplishments, heroes tangibly demonstrate that success is attainable totally within the human realm. When a job needs attention, Forrest is there, not behind a desk, but building boats. When a truck driver has a flat on Sunday and the shop is closed, he knows he can call Forrest. When a family is in need, Nina and the daughters provide food, clothing, or just plain country comfort. As Nina and Forrest prove every day, the hero symbolizes those qualities that make the company special and unique.

On a recent occasion, an irate customer called Ranger on a Saturday morning expecting to unload on an employee. He voiced his complaint to the individual and then demanded to talk to "Mr. Ranger." The employee said, "This is Forrest Wood." The minor problem was handled over the phone, and the customer had a nice weekend with his Ranger.

Recently, a Ranger owner stopped at the plant unannounced and his tour guide was Forrest Wood. As they toured the plant, the visiting boat owner commented about a Ranger boat part he had broken. Forrest rummaged through the parts department and handed the owner a replacement.

By these acts Forrest and Nina reinforce the attention to detail and prompt service that make Ranger a successful business and the leading boat manufacturer. With ingenuous conduct toward customers, employees, and suppliers, they shape the corporate culture, establish its values, and, through rituals, create and reinforce its tradition.

At Ranger the people have a profit sharing program simply because Forrest and Nina believe, "Our people have given the best part of their life to Ranger and we want them to know that we appreciate their efforts."

While much of corporate America emphasizes the bottom line, often at the expense of employees, consumers, and product quality, the Woods emphasize people and product quality. "If you take care of your people and treat them right and take care of the consumer by providing a quality product with excellent service, the bottom line will reflect it." For Ranger boats the bottom line is a consequence of doing things right; its not an end in and of itself.

Self-Confidence to Achieve

What the Woods have undertaken requires an enormous amount of self-confidence and unbending commitment. Like other entrepreneurs, often their efforts are questioned by others of less vision, which can create some lonely moments. "You know, the entrepreneur is really a lonely breed, but Nina and I have had each other, which has made it easier and has built a strong marriage. Most entrepreneurs are not necessarily happy because of the loneliness, and some of the happiest people I know work for other people." Nina states, "There's a great responsibility for our people and sometimes the burdens of our decisions are very heavy, like when we decided to 'bet the farm' and sell the guide business, we worked so hard for over fourteen years to rebuild Ranger and provide jobs for our neighbors."

The night of the fire, many of Flippin's residents believed Forrest and Nina would not recover, but as we have seen they spent that sleepless night plotting their way back. Facing overwhelming odds—90 percent of uninsured small businesses destroyed by fire never reopen—they moved forward. The offers for financial help from dealers, who pledged to pay for boats not yet built, reaffirmed their conviction and their decision. An employee comments, "If there was only one person in the world left without a boat, Forrest and Nina would be there to build a Ranger."

Their self-confidence in their ability to achieve is complemented by their talent to pick and motivate good people. Forrest states, "Our strongest asset is our ability to pick people who believe in the work ethic, are proud of a job well done, and who are self-motivated. Somehow I developed the ability to relate to people; I understand their wants, and I treat them with respect and appreciation. The world revolves around selling and that's promoting not just products, but ideas to motivate people and gain their commitment, particularly if they don't see the big picture."

This relationship with their people has gained them an unprecedented degree of loyalty, respect, and love. On one occasion, a truck driver suffered a massive heart attack and the Wood's plane was dispatched to bring the employee home. After a lengthy convalescence, the driver returned to work, and shortly thereafter a second attack killed him. As the family and friends paid their respects, Forrest was surprised to see that the employee's family had buried the driver in a Ranger "T"-shirt and had a Ranger truck etched in his marble tombstone. This expression of loyalty certainly is unusual, but it does speak to the belief that people who know them have in the Woods. "Forrest and Nina have a way of comforting you. When I have a problem, they know just what to say, and they always focus on the potential opportunity, not the problem itself," a worker states.

"You have to have the self-confidence to let go and give your people free reign, and we give them the authority to make decisions without reprisal," remark the Woods. At Ranger the decision making process is collective, with equal employee participation. "It always amazes me that Forrest and Nina never dictate, but they call us together and get our opinions. When the project is complete, I can see my part and the impact of others. Our opinions really count, and it gives us pride."

Says Forrest, "If you're right all the time then you can run a dictatorship, but if you're not, you better have the self-confidence to admit it and get other opinions. I am careful not to tell my people what I think because I really want their thoughts — not what they think I want to hear. In letting go and giving my people authority I am acknowledging that I can't be all things to all people and there's often somebody who can do the job as good or better than me."

Epilogue

Never having met Forrest and Nina Wood prior to our interview, we really didn't know what to expect. Telephone conversations to arrange the interview revealed a voice with a deep southern drawl and some degree of skepticism. I certainly did not expect to start the interview, which was held in rural Flippin, Arkansas, with Forrest insightfully expounding on international economics, global politics, and the general entrepreneurial operating environment. According to Forrest, "We live in a country where there are no limits, a country that will let us go as far as we want to. How far we excel, or how high we fly, depends on each individual."

He further stated, "We clearly are the land of opportunity, and we are at the crossroads where the ways of capitalism are appearing on a global scale. We saw evidence of this in Europe with the election of Margaret Thatcher and in America with the election of Ronald Reagan. The world realizes that capitalism is more efficient than the other 'isms,' but we have some major obstacles to free enterprise that need to be addressed in order to reestablish America's lead as the great business leader and bastion of capitalism."

Below are some of Forrest Woods thoughts on other subjects of interest to aspiring or practicing entrepreneurs.

On the legal profession: "Some attorneys have created a self-serving bureaucratic industry that hinders capitalistic progress. This is best evidenced by the insurance crisis, with product liability insurance killing the businessman. People ask me how long do Rangers last and I tell them I don't know. Many of our first boats are still in the water. Then we find ourselves a defendant in a product liability suit with a 1971 Ranger. The culprits were drunk and charged with DWI, but we got sued because the allegation was that our lights weren't working. The plaintiffs' attorneys alleged that there was a short in our wiring system that prevented the victims from seeing the Ranger boat lights. Well, if another boat hits any boat at fifty miles an hour, something's going to give!"

"The cost of insurance has been prohibitive and like many, we self-insure part of the risk. Even if we win the case we have expenses, and equally important is our time, while some attorney is looking for deep pockets. I hate to see limits placed on product liability claims because there are legitimate cases where damages are due, but so many cases are based on the ambulance-chasing greed of some attorneys. They have developed a self-serving economy based on contingencies, which certainly has its associated risks. Our entire economy is affected!"

On bureaucracy: "A major problem with corporate America is the bureaucracies that are established within a company. These are defeating to the collective effort. When some advance at the expense of others, people are actually competing against each other and building little empires; there's no family spirit of cooperation and the associated politics become the objective at the expense of efficiency, product quality, and consumer satisfaction. Management allows and encourages this with its numbers mentality and disregard for the human element. I guess they think that by pitting people against each other they are encouraging the survival of the fittest. It's not management's job to play mother nature, it has dangerous consequences. Can you imagine a bee hive being built by twenty different cliques all going separate ways to be the first to complete the project—it would never work and it doesn't work in companies; people need to work together. Bureaucracies waste resources, and most important, they lose the human element and management needs to introduce different work incentives."

On government: "Government's job is not to govern but to provide an environment that encourages business progress and the nourishment of new ideas. We have created a welfare mentality that threatens the basic principles of hard work and pride for a job well done. It's tragic when the main topic of conversation is how to get more welfare, it has destroyed the will to achieve. For decades we saw the impact of this treatment on the American Indian, and we see this cancer killing the human spirit today. In this way government has done the gravest disservice by eliminating human incentive."

Chapter 14

*Some Final
Thoughts on
Entrepreneurship*

Some Final Thoughts on Entrepreneurship

*I*n 1776, America declared its independence and Adam Smith wrote his economic treatise, *The Wealth of Nations*. He acknowledged the entrepreneur's efforts in marshalling land, labor, and capital. He also noted that, in addition to possessing a benign capitalistic greed, the entrepreneur is motivated by a host of unexplainable needs that he referred to as the "invisible hand." At the time, the definition of entrepreneur was: "Capital risk-taker." Two hundred plus years later the definition pretty much was the same and the particular characteristics that motivate the entrepreneur still remained a mystery.

During Adam Smith's time of "cottage industries," the term "capital risk taker" was distinguishing, since capital was limited and held by few. But as our economy evolved, capital has become more abundant and diversified and the activities of entrepreneurs have moved well beyond "capital risk taking" to the point where the definition no longer is very meaningful.

Based on our student research at Harvard, Stanford and Vanderbilt, on our surveys of 1,500 entrepreneurs and on our 13 interviews, we submit the following as a more appropriate definition of today's entrepreneur: *"Nature's emissary to enterprise who uses his or her vision and resourcefulness to exploit opportunity in the face of change."*

We refer to the entrepreneur as, *"nature's emissary to enterprise,"* because of the attributes he or she instinctively and *naturally* uses to exploit business opportunity. Although we are not able to ascertain whether the 12 entrepreneurial traits we were able to identify are inherited or learned characteristics, we do believe that they first surface in the entrepreneur's youth. The characteristics are often first developed as coping mechanisms in response to adversity and hardship faced in youth and are re-directed in adulthood to more positive entrepreneurial pursuits. We use the word "enterprise" broadly in our definition, by the way, to convey entrepreneurial opportunity in all arenas of social activity, including business, government, academia, not-for-profit, and so forth.

Our definition also refers to the entrepreneur's *"vision and resourcefulness to exploit opportunity in the face of change."* Periods of social and economic change provide opportunities to exploit. Great periods of change have occurred during Europe's Industrial Revolution and America's Technological Revolution and are occurring now, during our transition to an Information Society. As a result, entrepreneurial activity is re-emerging and is playing a dominant role in the restructuring of America's economy once again.

This re-emergence of today's entrepreneurial movement and its success is in evidence when one looks at the entrepreneur's role in creating new jobs in the U.S. over the last two decades. Since 1965, it is estimated that a total of 40 million new jobs were created in America, a phenomenal achievement that neither Japan nor Europe could come close to matching. During the same period, the largest U.S. companies, as a group, actually experienced a decline of 6 million employees, government employment also declined, and hospital and university employment remained relatively stable. The new jobs were created almost solely by thousands of small and mid-size entrepreneurial companies, many of which are in industries that did not even exist in 1965. It is further estimated that 80% of these 40 million new jobs were created by firms of 100 employees or less! It is now a fact that the entrepreneurial segment of our economy employs more people, pays more taxes, and produces more technological advancements than any other segment.

One concept that is conspicuously absent from our definition is any reference to "risk taking." During Adam Smith's day, the entrepreneur almost always had to risk his or her own capital because of the centralized control and limited availability of funds for business investment. In contrast, today's entrepreneur finds abundant and diversified sources of investment capital. And, although many entrepreneurs still risk their own capital on their new ventures, it has become less of a dominant issue. Those who are providing today's venture capital have become the primary risk-takers. The financial risk that attends any new enterprise has shifted, in great part, from the entrepreneur to the investor.

Unlike many other observers of the entrepreneurial scene, we are not convinced that the 12 entrepreneurial characteristics presented in this book can be taught and successfully implemented in the same way that management skills can. Just as universities cannot teach wisdom, we do not believe that they can effectively impart to their students such qualities as vision, resourcefulness, independence, perserverence, etc. By the time a person reaches college age, either these traits are well established and operating or they are not and never will be.

Despite having said this, we now will argue in favor of teaching entrepreneurship in our schools for two fundamental reasons:

1) For those students who may possess entrepreneurial traits, exposure to the subject at an early age may sensitize them to entrepreneurial opportunities sooner than they otherwise would be.

2) And, a society that is generally more knowledgeable about entrepreneurship, its benefits as well as its requirements, may more fully appreciate and encourage entrepreneurial pursuits.

Intrapreneurship   Although we seem to be engaged in a major transformation toward an entrepreneurial economy, we are skeptical of corporate America's ability to adopt and incorporate entrepreneurship as it claims to be doing through the recent emergence of "intrapreneurship." The reasons for our skepticism are simple: for the most part, corporate America embraces and encourages organizational principles that are counter to the free-spirited ideals of the entrepreneur. Similarly, corporate America does not encourage or adapt well to change, the vital ingredient needed to stimulate entrepreneurship. And, lastly, the short-term, return-on-investment mentality of the widely held public company is counter to the long-run, quarterly-profits-be-damned management approach of the entrepreneur.

This is not to say that small or mid-size companies have a monopoly on entrepreneurship, for their are several large public companies that truly are entrepreneurial. But, we do believe that it is the smaller companies that are finding it easier to embrace an entrepreneurial operating approach on a large scale. The larger corporations, before they can make this shift to a more entrepreneurial management style, to any great degree, first will have to undergo massive internal cultural changes to shed themselves of deeply ingrained bureaucratic attitudes and static operating styles. This will require extensive restructurings of companies and even entire industries, which, as the business press informs us daily, already is underway. For an insightful and more in depth look at this phenomenon, Peter Drucker's book, *Innovation and Entrepreneurship* (Harper & Row) is recommended reading.

The Entrepreneurial Society   One measure of society's increasing support of entrepreneurship is its greater allocation of available investment funds to entrepreneurial pursuits. In the sixties and seventies, primarily due to restrictive tax policies and other government policies, fewer dollars were being allocated to venture capital. By contrast, venture capital funds in the eighties have amassed assets in the billions of dollars. Although this still may be a small amount relative to other available investment opportunities, the increase in available venture capital has helped fuel, and is a reflection of, the movement towards an entrepreneurial economy.

Ironically, our society, which, as we have argued above, benefits greatly from entrepreneurship (just think of the burden on federal, state and local government welfare and unemployment benefit systems if small business had not created those 40 million new jobs since 1965), is also, in many ways, the entrepreneur's greatest obstacle. Society, like the bureaucratic corporation we spoke of before, encourages order, structure, conformity, and the *status quo.* It similarly discourages the free-spirited, independent style of the entrepreneur. We believe, however, that this will change, and, in fact, is already beginning to. As the social benefits that result from entrepreneurship are more widely disseminated to all segments of our population (which, we hope, this book will have some small part in doing), future generations of Americans will be more sensitive to the needs of this truly rare and particularly American form of business organization. As this trend widens and continues in the next decades and as America's future generations of labor talent become even more accustomed to the benefits that accrue to entrepreneurship, the corporate transition from a predominately bureaucratic managerial system to an entrepreneurial one will finally reach fruition. *(Re-Inventing the Corporation,* Naisbitt and Aburdene).

However, as we have touched on in various places in the preceding chapters, in order for this transition to take place, we must undertake some major reevaluations of our past business attitudes and practices. Some of the more obvious of these are summarized below:

1) The short-term, quarter-to-quarter investment mentality of the stock market must give way to new longer-term and more qualitative measures of performance.

2) Corporate America must decentralize into smaller, more autonomous and accountable operating units.

3) Companies must better take into account the personal needs of all their constituents, including their employees, customers, suppliers and shareholders; and more openly interact with and be accountable to society as a whole.

4) Corporate managers must learn not to discourage failure in their organizations, but accept it as a normal learning process.

5) Change must be encouraged, actively pursued in fact, and rewarded.

6) Corporations must complete the transition from a Theory X management climate, in which it is assumed that labor requires autocratic supervision, to the more enlightened Theory Y approach, in which employees are given the autonomy to reach (or not) their full potential on their own.

7) Corporate rigidity and conformance must give way to a more flexible, informal and open operating environment.

8) Corporate America must put more emphasis on entrepreneurship, which must be more fully reflected in the culture, rituals, and reward systems of individual companies. Large corporations must more fully share in the risks and rewards of entrepreneurship.

9) Companies must become more market oriented, responding more directly to fulfilling individual customer needs as opposed to meeting internal production requirements.

10) The role of money and profits must be recognized as a means to an end and not the sole purpose of enterprise.

A Collective View   Although we reviewed scores of periodicals, statistical studies, books and research papers for this project, we paid particular attention to four publications: Deal and Kennedy's, *Corporate Cultures;* Peter Drucker's, *Innovation and Entrepreneurship;* George Gilder's, *The Spirit of Enterprise;* and Naisbitt and Aburdene's *Re-Inventing The Corporation.* These works, as does this one, address the circumstances and impact of the transformation of America's work environment from a managerial culture, spawned by the Industrial Revolution, to an entrepreneurial culture, engendered by the Information Revolution. In all four books, the central and common character is the entrepreneur. Below are some pertinent excerpts from these four books that support the general themes of this author.

According to Naisbitt and Aburdene, "We are living in one of those rare times in history when the two crucial elements for social change are present—new values and economic necessity." The authors emphasize that these new values are being promoted by the emerging baby boom work force, which is, "The most entrepreneurial generation in this nation's history." According to the authors, in order for corporate America to attract this generation of workers, it "must create an environment that is nourishing to the entrepreneurs."

Likewise, according to Peter Drucker, "What is happening in the United States is a profound shift from a 'managerial' to an 'entrepreneurial' economy. So far, the entrepreneurial economy is purely an American Phenomenon."

Allen Kennedy, co-author of *Corporate Cultures,* remarks that "large corporations as we know them will not exist in thirty years." He believes that these companies, as presently structured, will not be able to hold on to their people, and especially their more talented ones, because too many will strike out on their own. Kennedy's advice to corporate America is to create a culture that encourages and rewards entrepreneurship to attract and retain good people.

And, finally, George Gilder in *The Spirit of Enterprise* states, "The entrepreneurs' role is to generate entirely new markets or theories. In this, they are limited only by the compass of their own imagination and powers of persuasion... They bring entirely new things into the world in a process that they themselves control.''

These eminent authors offer convincing evidence consistent with my own beliefs that America is in the process of converting to an entrepreneurial economy. The elements of this change include a shift from a capital intensive economy to one that is information based, from a solely profit-oriented business approach to one that stresses quality and value, from a numbers driven culture to one that is people oriented, and, from an autocratic and bureaucratic corporate style to one that is humanistic. These changes are being led and driven first and foremost by the Rare Breed, the entrepreneurs we met and studied in this book.

In order to help facilitate this inevitable transition and promote better understanding of the needs and motivations of the entrepreneur, we have tried to shed some light on the traits that drive these unique business people. It was hoped that by identifying these traits and by showing how they have shaped the lives and careers of successful, living, breathing people, the reader would gain a better understanding and appreciation of this remarkable American phenomenon—the entrepreneur. We have attempted to eliminate the mystique surrounding the entrepreneur by providing both definition and example.

What is vitally important for all of us who care about the future of this country to understand and appreciate is that America, with its uniquely free social, political, and economic environment is the best, and possibly the only, true breeding ground for this rare species of individual. The entrepreneur is our heritage and our future. It is in all our best interests to perpetuate the species. Our continued evolution as an economically free and vital nation may well depend on it.

Bill MacPhee

REFERENCES

General

Terrence E. Deal and Allan A. Kennedy, *Corporate Cultures* (Massachusetts: Addison Wesley, 1982).

Peter Drucker, *Innovation and Entrepreneurship* (New York: Harper and Row, 1985).

Harold Geneen, *Managing* (Garden City, New York: Doubleday, 1984).

Geoge Gilder, *The Spirit of Enterprise* (New York: Simon and Schuster, 1984).

John Naisbitt and Patricia Aburdene, *Re-Inventing the Corporation* (New York: Warner Books, September 1985).

Dennis Waitley, *The Psychology of Winning* (New York: Berkeley Publishing Group, 1984).

Chapter Two

Mary Kay Ash, *Mary Kay* (New York: Barnes & Noble, 1981).

Mary Kay Ash, *Mary Kay on People Management* (New York: Warner Books, 1984).

Chapter Four

Helen F. Boehm, *With A Little Luck* (New York: Rawson and Associates, 1985).

Frank Cosentine, *Edward Marshall Boehm 1913-1969* (Chicago: R.R. Donnelley & Son, 1970).